ANGRY VOICES

KENNIKAT PRESS SCHOLARLY R' 'RINTS

Dr. Ralph Adams Brown, Senior Editor

Series in
AMERICAN HISTORY AND CULTURE
IN THE TWENTIETH CENTURY
Under the General Editorial Supervision of
Dr. Donald R. McCoy
Professor of History, University of Kansas

ANGRY VOICES

*Left-of-Center Politics in the
New Deal Era*

by

Donald R. McCoy

KENNIKAT PRESS
Port Washington, N. Y./London

77- 7765

ANGRY VOICES

Copyright 1958 by The University of Kansas Press
Reissued in 1971 by Kennikat Press by arrangement
Libray of Congress Catalog Card No: 78-137975
ISBN 0-8046-1431-8

Manufactured by Taylor Publishing Company   Dallas, Texas

KENNIKAT SERIES ON AMERICAN HISTORY AND
CULTURE IN THE TWENTIETH CENTURY

PREFACE

The commanding figure of the 1930's was undoubtedly Franklin Delano Roosevelt. Whether interpreted as hero, villain, or a mixture of both, this man and his activities have almost exclusively dominated the writings of the political historians of the period. Yet this preoccupation with the "great man" constitutes only the beginning of serious probing of New Deal era politics. American politics has always been based on diversity of interest and character. It has represented a series of vigorous contests for power. The 1930's were no exception; the decade served as a battleground for a great variety of political forces. These elements were not just "also rans." To the right and left of the President and even in his own camp, they struggled to influence the course of legislation and administration. It seems fair to say that until these forces are studied, full understanding of American politics in the 1930's will be lacking.

My specific task in this book has been to probe to the left of Roosevelt and his immediate associates, hoping to recapture the essence of the thought, action, and psychology of those of so-called left-wing orientation. I have sought not so much to narrate or to judge their successes and failures in influencing government policies, as to shed more light on the dynamics of American politics in the depression decade.

There are two great difficulties in dealing with left-of-center politics in the 1930's. The first concerns phraseology. Terms like "left-wing," "left-of-center," "liberal," "progressive," and "radical" are troublesome not only because they have been vested by previous writers with emotional connotations, but also because they lack any concrete definition. Yet these terms are an integral part of the vocabulary of the 1930's and therefore cannot be ignored in an historical study of the period. As used in this book, "left-wing" and "left-of-center" merely describe groups and persons demanding more governmental action in dealing with political problems than advocated at the time by the two major parties. Words like "liberal," "progressive," and "radical" are used to describe any group or individual as it described itself or its program at a given time, though of course it was not unusual for a group or person to use at the same time two or all three of these terms in self-description. Such terms are herein used only for their limited descriptive value and not in any derogatory sense.

The second great difficulty in dealing with the left-of-center forces of the 1930's is coping with their multiplicity. The American Laborites, Commonwealthers, Epicites, Farmer-Laborites, Progressives, and Socialists comprise only a small portion of the roster. To simplify the organization of this book, I have concentrated my attention on four groups which worked to amalgamate the left-wing elements into a new national party of significance. These organizations—the League for Independent Political Action, the Farmer-Labor or American Commonwealth Political Federation, the Union party, the National Progressives of America—afford a fairly serviceable framework for explaining left-of-center political activity in the 1930's because of their contacts with every important left-wing group in the country.

I make no claim to completeness in dealing with the subject of this book. A subject so rich in variety as this will allow future research to add much interesting and important material. Yet, for that which I have been able to do, I owe a great debt of gratitude to the many people who have helped me. I should especially like to thank the many participants and observers of the political struggles of the 1930's who helped me for their aid and advice. The high level of co-operation and assistance given by the staffs of the following institutions is most gratefully acknowledged: the Library of Congress, the State Historical Society of Wisconsin, the Minnesota Historical Society, the Franklin D. Roosevelt Library, the Cornell University Library, the University of Chicago Library, the University of Kansas Library, the Houghton Library at Harvard University, and the St. Bonaventure University Library. I should like to thank the University of Kansas for a grant from its Research Fund which was of material assistance in completing this study. Chapter VII of this book is based substantially on my article in Volume XLIV of the *Mississippi Valley Historical Review;* I greatly appreciate the courtesy of the *Review's* editors in granting me permission to use this article. No list of acknowledgments would be complete without referring to those without whose encouragement and suggestions this book would not have been written: Arthur A. Ekirch and Ernst Posner of the American University, Louis Hunter of the Armed Forces Industrial College, the late Everett Edwards of the United States Department of Agriculture, and especially my wife, Vivian Rogers McCoy. I am, of course, solely responsible for any errors of fact and judgment to be found in this book.

DONALD R. McCOY

Lawrence, Kansas

CONTENTS

CONTENTS

Chapter I
PRAGMATIC DISCONTENT

The advocates of left-wing protest in the 1930's could look back upon a rich political heritage. Beginning with John Randolph's "Tertium Quid," dissident political movements had not failed, for any substantial length of time, to challenge the supremacy of the major political parties. The Workingmen's parties of the 1820's and 1830's, the Free Soilers, the welter of farmer and labor parties after the Civil War, the Populists, the various Socialist groups, and the 1912 Progressive party contributed to the tradition of organized protest politics in the United States.

In 1912 a high water mark was established with third-party candidates polling 35 per cent of the total vote for President. Yet, four years later, the liberal accomplishments of the Wilson administration and the precarious position of the nation in world affairs combined to lessen drastically not only the appeal of third-party action but of progressivism and radicalism. American participation in World War I struck an even more telling blow. Progressives like Robert M. La Follette, Sr., and George Norris were stigmatized as pawns of German imperialism; Eugene V. Debs and other Socialists were imprisoned for their political activities; the Nonpartisan League and the Industrial Workers of the World were vigorously assaulted as revolutionary and un-American organizations. The end of war brought no relief. The attacks

1

of "100 per cent Americans" upon "subversive" elements continued unabated. Economic and social conservatism dominated both major parties. Even worse, bickering among radical and progressive leaders, as illustrated in the failure of the Farmer-Labor party of 1920, rose to new heights.

Encouraged by new stirrings of discontent in 1920-1921 and by the successes of the British Labour party, American protest leaders sought to fuse various dissident elements into one movement. This effort resulted, in 1922, in the launching of the Conference for Progressive Political Action by organized labor, Socialists, Nonpartisan Leaguers, intellectuals, and social gospel forces. The Conference resolved to make a major bid for national political power in 1924 by encouraging and supporting the presidential candidacy of Robert M. La Follette, Sr. Although hampered by lack of campaign funds and by amateurism in the ranks, he polled almost five million votes, one-sixth of those cast. Yet despite this admirable showing, the third-party coalition soon began to fall apart, largely as a result of disappointment with defeat. The disintegration of the Conference for Progressive Political Action and the nation's increasing economic prosperity resulted in a precipitous decline of protest politics. In 1928, third-party presidential candidates attracted less than 400,000 ballots —the smallest percentage of the popular vote cast for third-party standard-bearers since 1872. The Democratic nominee, Alfred E. Smith of New York, drew support from most of the country's urban liberals,

while agrarians generally decided to take a chance
with Herbert Hoover. The rural progressives nominally remained in the Republican camp for a few
years after 1928. The campaign, however, offered
proof for most urban liberals that Republicanism
could not be reformed, and left many of them with
the feeling that further work in the Democratic party
would be wasted.

Out of this disillusionment came the first active
movement in the 1930's to form a consolidated left-
of-center party. The movement was prefaced by a
stirring call to action by that venerable organ of protest, the *Nation*. The magazine declared that "the
Democratic high tide of votes in 1928 was not due to
party principles. . . . Nor was it in response to any
thrilling new—or old—social or international program, for no such program was presented." The large
Democratic vote was interpreted as being caused by
resentment at the slander of Smith's origins, religion,
views on prohibition, and "such liberalism as he
voiced." Millions of citizens, it was asserted, were
politically homeless. "Opposed to the Republican
party, they cannot embrace the Democratic now
that it insists that it, too, stands for Big Business, for
high tariffs, for the gospel of all-controlling prosperity, for the curtailment of immigration, for a big
navy, and has forgotten all about the Wilsonian doc-
trines of 1912." In view of the apparent intellectual
bankruptcy of the Democratic party, the *Nation* demanded that a liberal political party be prepared to

3

step onto the national scene regardless of the difficulties involved. "The way to begin is to begin."[1]

The *Nation's* editorial represented the thinking of those who were convinced that dissent should be organized as well as verbalized. To accomplish this, the League for Independent Political Action was established in September, 1929, to work for the formation of a new political party.[2] The leadership of the League was distinguished. John Dewey, then America's most famed thinker, was selected chairman. The vice chairmen were James H. Maurer, President of the Pennsylvania Federation of Labor and 1928 Socialist candidate for Vice President of the United States; Zona Gale, who was in the forefront of the novelists of social criticism; and a rising young professor of economics in the University of Chicago, Paul H. Douglas. Oswald Garrison Villard, editor of the *Nation,* was treasurer, and Howard Y. Williams, a Unitarian clergyman, was executive secretary. Among those serving on the national executive committee were Paul Brissenden, Nathan Fine, Harry W. Laidler, Robert Morss Lovett, Reinhold Niebuhr, and B. C. Vladeck. The National Committee included Paul Blanshard, Stuart Chase, John Haynes Holmes, John Ise, W. E. B. DuBois, and Alexander Meiklejohn.[3] Fashioned in the light of these intellectuals, the League for Independent Political Action was designed to be bold and honest in its actions, comprehensive and intelligent in its implications for change.

4

The basic line of criticism adopted by the new organization was economic. Particularly distressing to the League's founders was "the unequal distribution of the national income, whereby a few have a surfeit while great numbers live below the standard that conservative research bureaus deem sufficient." Independent political action was demanded because neither of the two major parties gave any evidence of being concerned with this situation. In political terms, it was contended that it was impossible for progressives to capture the major parties and that to remain within either would necessitate continued compromise of liberal principles. The League pointed out that a liberal could neither with impunity stay within a major party and support other parties' candidates, nor with effect switch from party to party to support candidates with similar viewpoints. It was also held that a united progressive party could better stand desertions and treachery than could a liberal movement divided by a multitude of partisan and factional loyalties.[4] LIPA, therefore, proposed "a new political alignment whereby economic progressives will leave the old parties to the conservatives, and will together with those already outside the old parties unite to build a new party based on the principle of increased social planning and control."[5]

The League made a comparison between the founding of the Republican party and the inevitability of a new, liberal-radical party. Just as the former rose out of the battle against chattel slavery, the new

5

party was to be born out of the struggle to free the people from enslavement by "selfish and predatory" economic interests.[6] Disavowing any intention of becoming the new party itself, LIPA sought to serve as the fostering parent of a party representative of hand and brain workers, farmers, and all those who were dissatisfied with major party policies. To achieve this end, the League established itself as a clearing house for the activities of groups and individuals seeking political realignment; it conducted research work, carried on a vigorous campaign of educational publicity, and lent aid to organizational activities.[7] In the research area, committees of experts were soon formed to develop effective solutions to the country's domestic and foreign problems, with the following major goals in mind: to bring public utilities, transportation, and communication "more adequately under social control"; to "democratize industry"; to achieve "greater equalization of incomes"; to establish national standards of health and recreation; to provide accident, health, unemployment, and old-age insurance for all; to legalize collective bargaining; to reduce tariffs; to encourage co-operative enterprises; to establish a system of farm credits and insurance; to provide for a more just system of Congressional representation; to restore full civil liberties to minority groups; and to prevent war.[8] These goals and the proposed solutions thereto were to be thoroughly discussed by the League's membership before they were to be presented to the public.

6

The spectacular collapse of business activities in the United States, starting in October, 1929, buttressed the charges, facts, figures, and possible solutions which LIPA publicized. As a result of the coming of the depression, many observers felt that the future looked auspicious for independent political action and especially so for the League. Of the three significant national organizations of political dissent —the Communist party, the Socialist party, and the League for Independent Political Action—the third was closest to the inherent caution and conservatism of the American people. The League had been conceived within the fold of a native philosophy, and was staffed with people familiar to the intellectual and politically sophisticated segments of the nation. LIPA was also fortunately free from the foreign connections of the Communist party, unburdened by an unpopular name, and unencumbered by a history of violence and mud-slinging. Yet the League was akin to the proverbial boy sent to do a man's job. Its local organizations were all but nonexistent and a definite platform had not been formulated.

In 1930, LIPA strove valiantly to educate the American people to the "necessity" of militant but intelligent political action. Its positions on current issues were widely publicized through leaflets, press releases, and articles in key magazines of comment and intellect. The League's officials worked energetically to assist the growth of grass roots independent political action groups. Progressive candidates for public office, regardless of party, were endorsed

7

and supported. The results of these efforts were mildly encouraging. During its first nine months of operation, the League had enlisted 2,500 dues-paying members. It had participated in the formation of a number of local independent parties, some of which successfully ran candidates for office.[9] In Minnesota, the League was heartened by the election of Farmer-Laborites as governor and United States senator.

After the 1930 elections, LIPA launched an experiment designed to induce members of the progressive bloc in Congress to lend their support to the movement for a new party. The Congressional progressives, although few in numbers, were able and vocal and had the confidence of millions of citizens. The League devised the strategy of trying first to convert the leading Congressional progressive, Senator George W. Norris of Nebraska, hoping that his colleagues would follow him. It was thought that the possibility of converting Norris would be enhanced by the fact that he had just undergone a particularly irksome campaign for re-election, and, in addition, had been read out of the Republican party by the executive director of its National Committee.[10] On Christmas Day, 1930, John Dewey wrote to Norris asking if he would not "renounce both of these old parties and help give birth to a new party based upon the principle of planning and control for the purpose of building happier lives, a more just society and that peaceful world which was the dream of Him whose birthday we celebrate this Christmas Day." Dewey prophesied that a liberal party repre-

8

senting the interests of the people could win the Presidency by 1940. "We could drive the conservatives in desperation into one of the old parties and we should then have a real conflict of ideas and a vital party of opposition which would make for rapid political progress and give desperate workers and farmers a constructive vehicle of political expression."[11] Norris' reply was prompt. He agreed with Dewey's indictment of the two old parties and with the need for social legislation. He could not see that such legislation could be obtained by organizing a third party. Norris felt that a new party could arouse public sympathy only after the major party conventions had met. "The time is then too short . . . and the expense is too great." To Norris, no political party could avoid being accompanied by patronage, coercion, evasion, and skulduggery. As his biographers observed, the Nebraska Senator "admired the altruism of men like Dewey and Williams, but thought independent voting the solution."[12] John Dewey, after receiving his reply, asserted that men like Norris "continue to snipe and occasionally bring down some game that should be, heaven knows, gotten out of the way." Dewey charged that the progressives in Congress were impractical in thinking they were ever going to achieve anything of importance without facing the fundamental issue of whether the people or the plutocrats were to control government.[13]

The dramatic Dewey-Norris exchange had some value to LIPA. It gained an unusually large amount of attention in the nation's press for the organization's objectives. More important, the affair seemed to give credence to Paul Douglas' later observation that to chase the "good man" in an old party was to flirt with the danger of forming a jerry-built progressive party. Douglas recommended that the League concentrate on constructing a "solid political organization rooted in integrity and principle, which can stand by itself. When this is done, good men . . . [will] come to the organization of the progressive forces for the protection and aid which only such a group can give."[14] The episode had other reverberations. It marked a temporary split between LIPA and the Conference for Progressive Labor Action, an organization which had been formed to act in the economic sphere much as the League hoped to function in the political arena. A. J. Muste, chairman of the Conference and later head of the Trotskyite American Workers' party, announced his resignation from LIPA's executive committee. He charged that the Dewey-Norris correspondence revealed the League's goal to be a liberal party. "Something more drastic and coherent is required," Muste asserted. "A loosely constructed party, with a nice program built around a few individuals and including groups with diverse economic interests, would get us nowhere."[15] The Dewey-Norris exchange also probably contributed to continued lack of co-operation between LIPA and the progressive bloc in Congress. This lack was well illustrated by the failure of the Congressional progressives to invite the League to participate in their Conference of Progressives in 1931. In fact, the call to the conference and the remarks of its chairman, Senator Norris, stressed opposition to "any intention or idea of organizing a third or independent party."[16] Some comfort for LIPA leaders was, however, to be derived from the conversion of the *New Republic* to their cause. The liberal magazine called for the development of a new party to replace one of the old parties "while the door is open." To supplement its new editorial policy, the *New Republic* announced that Professor Dewey would write a series of four articles on the need for a new party.[17]

During 1931, LIPA's committees of experts continued the study and formulation of proposed solutions to the economic, political, and social problems of the United States. An increasing flow of pamphlets and magazine articles were issued by the League's authors. Utilizing radio and the lecture hall, teams of LIPA orators endeavored to acquaint the people with the chief issues. Contacts were made with influential liberals and progressives, whether in or out of office. Aid and encouragement were given to the establishment of state and local third parties. In organizing units of the League, its leaders continued to make progress. By 1932, LIPA had eight state coordinating committees, forty-seven city branches, and organizers in forty-two other cities. The League also made strenuous efforts to achieve official joint action with the Socialist and Minnesota Farmer-Labor parties.[18] Although these groups evaded commitment on the formation of a united party of lib-

11

erals and radicals, individual Socialists were permitted by their party to participate in LIPA, and the Minnesota party's newspaper stated that the League "merits the support of all practical persons who honestly desire to see a new national party launched."[19]

One of the many problems with which the League had to contend was the plethora of new groups aspiring to the job of being "the" third party in 1932. In giving partial endorsement to LIPA, the Minnesota Farmer-Labor party organization had branded these other organizations as "premature," and stated that "their actions tend to bring the undertaking into ridicule and increases the difficulty of organizing a representative movement."[20] These allegations were borne out by the 1932 campaign. One example can be cited in the National Farmer-Labor party.[21] Claiming to be descendant from the Populists, this party had sponsored Frank E. Webb's presidential candidacy in 1928 and received 6,390 votes. Webb was renominated for President on April 27, 1932. In June he was purged from candidacy by the National Farmer-Labor party's executive committee because of his refusal to abide by the party's platform, which seemed little different from that of the Populists. Senator Huey Long was asked to replace him. Long refused the invitation, and on July 10 the party named as its standard-bearer "General" Jacob S. Coxey, the famous veteran of the fight for unemployment relief in the 1890's. Coxey was to receive 7,309 votes in November. Also entering the picture

12

was a dissident National Farmer-Laborite faction which had dubbed itself the Nationalist party. George I. Wilson was the party's presidential candidate. One of Wilson's first actions was to seek reconciliation with the National Farmer-Labor party. When his party disagreed with him upon refitting the splinter into the original chip, Wilson resigned his candidacy. His replacement, Seymour E. Allen, also resigned later in the campaign because of the party's non-recognition of labor problems and its failure to take a stand on the prohibition question. This marked the end of the Nationalists.[22]

Then there was the Jobless party founded by Father James R. Cox of Pittsburgh. Father Cox had made the headlines in January, 1932, by leading over 5,000 unemployed persons to Washington to demonstrate for passage of federal relief legislation. Soon after the march on Washington, Cox, in an address to an estimated 55,000 persons in Pittsburgh, predicted the rise of a new party with himself as a candidate for President unless federal aid to the jobless was enacted.[23] In April, the priest announced that a convention of the "army" of the unemployed would be held in St. Louis on August 17. The members of the "army" were to wear blue shirts and were to be organized into a political party of the jobless. Cox warned that the "Blue Shirts" would nominate a candidate for President on a radical platform unless relief was forthcoming by the date of the convention. He claimed that the movement had one million adherents already and asserted that more than a million

13

would attend the Jobless party assembly at St. Louis.[24] Father Cox launched his campaign while on a trip to Europe, calling for the conscription of wealth, state administration of all banks, and establishment of a comprehensive public works program. Now counting on the allegiance of seventeen million voters, the Pittsburgh priest declared that the United States had only two choices: "Either my party or communism."[25] Meanwhile, Frank E. Webb had assumed leadership of the newly founded Liberty party, the "coalition third party." Webb was later replaced by William H. Harvey, author of the well-known *Coin's Financial School,* after Webb's claim of Socialist support had been repudiated.[26] By the time of Father Cox's St. Louis convention, the Jobless and Liberty parties had agreed to join forces. In St. Louis, however, Cox and Harvey were unable to agree on who should be the presidential candidate of the joint organization. Consequently, the coalition split apart, with 500 persons attending the priest's convention and 500 rallying around Harvey's headquarters. Cox and Harvey were, of course, to become the respective presidential candidates of the Jobless and Liberty parties.[27] In September, the priest's campaign party was stranded in New Mexico owing to lack of funds. Three weeks later, Cox issued a statement saying that he had quit the stump because of pecuniary problems and to avoid a breakdown: he insisted, however, that he was still a candidate.[28] In the elections, Cox's vote was negligible, although 53,425 citizens cast their ballots for Harvey.

14

Far more important as a problem to the League for Independent Political Action was the rising possibility of the nomination of Governor Franklin D. Roosevelt of New York to head the national Democratic ticket. Almost alone among potential Democratic candidates, Roosevelt could appeal to liberals and progressives. He had an acceptable liberal record; he had a famous family name; and he had revealed prowess as a campaigner. The League recognized that Roosevelt's candidacy for President would severely hamper efforts to start a new progressive party in 1932. As early as October, 1931, LIPA attempted to make the public aware of Roosevelt's political defects. It was asserted that his selection by the Democrats would strike a great blow to the progressive cause. "He is not . . . a real liberal." He "has no adequate or well-thought-out policy on any of the large issues." The Governor was accused of bowing to Tammany Hall and of being responsible for an ineffectual and poorly conceived state relief program.[29] This method of assailing Roosevelt was soon changed by one of LIPA's spokesmen, Paul Douglas. Instead of attacking Roosevelt's "dubious liberalism," Douglas praised him, but with serious reservations. He contended that should the Governor be elected, he would be virtually helpless. "The Democratic party will remain the Democratic party under his administration. Since the local machines are founded upon local spoils, it will be impossible by federal appointments greatly to change the complexion of the party." This argument was carried even further by

15

asserting that the natural goal of a new President is re-election and that this calls for mollification of the local machines to gain renomination and election support. "Even the warmest admirers of Governor Roosevelt can hardly proclaim him to be of such heroic mold as to defy the political fates."[30]

Early in 1932, the relationship between the League and the Socialist party began to crystallize. Norman Thomas and LIPA, in separate statements made in February, had called for a comprehensive third party in the United States similar to the British Labour party.[31] The following month, John Dewey declared that unless a truly progressive nominee were offered by one of the major parties, a liberal-radical third party would most certainly be started. Norman Thomas and Morris Hillquit, representing the official viewpoint of the Socialist party, balked at concurring with Dewey's pronouncement. They flatly stated that a third party in 1932 would not receive Socialist support as had the Conference for Progressive Political Action in 1924. Thomas felt that a revolt at such a late date "would be another wasted effort as far as building a party is concerned. It would have less hope for ultimate success than the La Follette coalition, which did have some definitely organized working-class support."[32] Undoubtedly, Thomas and Hillquit were thinking in terms of avoiding a repetition of the blow which the Socialist party had suffered as a result of its co-operation in the 1924 Progressive campaign.[33] The only other organization of political consequence to which the

16

League could look for help in starting a new national party in 1932 was the Minnesota Farmer-Labor party. Many Farmer-Laborites were sympathetic to LIPA objectives, but they were committed to a policy of caution. It was asserted that the circumstances must be favorable for the launching of a new party and that the Minnesota party must be securely established in office.[34] With the development of general liberal support of Roosevelt's bid for the Democratic nomination, the Minnesota Farmer-Labor leaders were increasingly cool to LIPA's overtures. They were, very simply, fearful of losing strength to a rejuvenated state Democratic party. By spring of 1932, it was evident that the Farmer-Labor leaders and the Roosevelt forces had reached an informal agreement on mutual aid in the event of the New York Governor's nomination for President.[35] In addition to having lost Socialist and Minnesota Farmer-Labor support, the League had not been able to persuade the Congressional progressives that third-party action was necessary to secure liberal ends. Most of the members of the progressive bloc found Roosevelt acceptable as a liberal presidential candidate. Under the leadership of George Norris, they supported the New Yorker during the 1932 campaign.[36]

By May, LIPA could only jettison the new-party idea for 1932. Indicative of this were the instructions of the executive committee chairman to the delegates of the League's 1932 convention. The chores of the meeting were to include the selection of candidates

17

for "endorsement," and the drafting of a strong program for post-election action. The endorsement of
Norman Thomas for President was recommended to
the delegates.[37]

Although the League was forced to abandon
formation of a new party in 1932, it developed considerable enthusiasm in the presentation of its platform. This was in line with the organization's con-
tention that the new party, when finally founded,
would have to be formed around a definite program
rather than around candidates. The basis for this
idea was that American third parties had been historically built around the appeal of candidates, and
that when these men passed from the political picture the movements collapsed.[38] The platform of the
League for Independent Political Action was called
the Four-Year Presidential Plan. It was the product
of several years of labor by the League's committees
of experts, and contained policy recommendations
for the distant future as well as demands for implementation within the next four years. The Four-
Year Presidential Plan was devised with two purposes
in mind: either that of being the platform of any
party which should result from LIPA's activities, or
of being "stolen" by or forced upon the administration which was to take office the following year. This
dual purpose was basic to any program which LIPA
and its successor organizations formulated.[39]

The Four-Year Presidential Plan called for immediate relief of the working force from the consequences of the depression. It was recommended that

18

to aid the unemployed the federal government grant from three to five billion dollars for public works and appropriate annually at least $250,000,000 for direct relief. This program, along with other welfare state measures of the League, was to be financed by a sizable increase in higher-bracket income, corporation, and inheritance taxes. Labor was to be aided in gaining financial security by the removal of restrictions on its organizational activities and on collective bargaining, the implementation of workers' insurance and old-age pension plans with government contributions, and an expansion of the adult labor force through the abolition of child labor and the establishment of a six-hour day. The ability to gain a fair profit was to be restored to farmers through land tax reductions, revision of rural credits in favor of debtors, federal aid for co-operatives, and low interest federal farm financing. Increased economic democracy and service were demanded. To obtain these, a drastic limitation of stock speculation and a sweeping reorganization of the country's banking system were proposed. Immediate public ownership of the nation's power utilities and eventual public ownership of coal, oil, and railway properties were envisioned. In the attempt to gain greater political democracy and justice, efficient reorganizations of our national, state, and local governments and criminal codes were called for. Syndicalist and espionage laws were to be repealed, and statutes forbidding mob violence and lynching to be enacted.

19

To foster international trade, the Plan called for an immediate 25 per cent reduction in tariff rates and looked toward eventual free trade. It also demanded the establishment of a permanent world economic congress composed of delegates of labor, industry, commerce, agriculture, banking, and government. This congress was to oversee international financing and tariff reduction. To contribute to world peace, LIPA proposed the prohibition of conscription and of governmental subsidies to industries basic to war. Also recommended were American recognition of the Union of Soviet Socialistic Republics, repudiation of the German "war guilt" clause in the treaty of Versailles, and entrance into the World Court and the League of Nations. The Plan demanded the disavowal of the Roosevelt Corollary to the Monroe Doctrine, and the cancellation of inter-governmental debts in return for European co-operation in a universal disarmament program.[40]

The above discussion is but a bare sketch of the Four-Year Presidential Plan. The Plan was reminiscent of the Populist, Bull Moose, and 1924 Progressive platforms, and perhaps can be called the logical and more refined descendant of them. Although the LIPA platform was rambling in organization, it was, in 1932, the most comprehensive analysis of the nation's economic, political, and social needs to be proffered by a political group. It bore little resemblance to the truculent manifestoes of the Communist party; it represented a more practical and practicable form of idealism, in view of the verities of

20

American society, than did the programs of the Socialist party; and it was intended to repaint the American scene in strokes far more bold than those used by the New Deal.

In their oratory at the conference, the speakers attempted to deal more boldly and honestly with the situations facing the American people than major party orators. One of the main speakers, Oswald Garrison Villard, commenting on the contemporary scene, stated that even the Democrats and Republicans had finally "realized that the promise of a full dinner pail in the platforms would incite only ridicule, so they substituted the full beer mug." Villard also asserted that the Republican administration's relief program was essentially limited to its friends. This was witnessed in the lending of eighty million dollars by the Reconstruction Finance Corporation to Charles Dawes' bank a few days after his resignation as R.F.C. head. "But there is not one federal cent for a starving American citizen. . . . We are assured that we will continue under the good old American plan of letting unemployed workers seek private charity or starve." Another speaker, Howard Y. Williams, declared that the rank and file of citizens are determined to re-establish economic, political, and social democracy. "One finds this in the organization of the unemployed, the awakening of the farmers, the revolt of the miners, the bonus marchers, the auto workers and the 'blue shirts.' " It is more obvious than ever, Williams averred, that the "job-conscious and tired radicals" in Congress

21

cannot provide these popular stirrings with effective direction; new, energetic leadership is essential to gain social justice. Williams, along with the other major speakers of the conference, warned that either a people's party must be developed by 1936, or the possibility of a totalitarian regime in the United States must be faced.[41]

In special resolutions, the meeting adopted the recommendation of the LIPA executive committee to endorse the candidacy of Norman Thomas for President of the United States. "While we do not necessarily support every feature in the ultimate program of the Socialist party, we do believe that in the present election the candidacy and platform of Norman Thomas is infinitely preferable to those of other parties and we therefore urge all our members and friends to work and vote for him." The Conference also resolved by a vote of forty-seven branch delegations to eight not to support any candidates of the Communist party. The news was then disclosed that the Socialist party had adopted a proposal to allow its members to co-operate more closely with the League in the future. This spurred the determination of the LIPA conferees to attain their primary goal. The delegates therefore approved a call for a congress in 1933 to organize a new liberal party.[42] The conference was then adjourned and the editorial writers of the country took over to dissect the LIPA meeting.

The *Cleveland Plain Dealer* accorded the conference a warm welcome and excellent press coverage. It held that the idea of forming a third party was chimerical, although it agreed with many of the foreign policy and civil rights planks of the Four-Year Presidential Plan. Describing LIPA and its convention as a "healthful manifestation," the newspaper stated that "lusty criticism is the mainspring of political progress. A party or a system that cannot weather it deserves to die."[43] The *New York Times* scored the plans of LIPA as unrealistic. "Professor Dewey feels that 'the constituency is waiting; the response is waiting.' Most of us—and majorities are said by some advanced thinkers to be always wrong—will surmise that the League is waiting and may have a long wait. . . . Government by two parties is accepted by the great mass of Americans as indispensable."[44] The *New Republic,* because of what it felt to be the negligible differences between the League and the Socialist party, lauded the endorsement of Norman Thomas by LIPA as revealing "an acute sense of political reality."[45] On the other hand, William Leach in the *Christian Century* found the Cleveland meeting disappointing, criticizing LIPA for its apparent inability to "lead the social and political liberals out of [their] present day impasse." Leach pointed out that there were two wings of the progressive movement: the academics, and the "unschooled radicals" of the laboring classes. He contended that it was doubtful whether the intellectual LIPA would ever become truly representative of both groups.[46]

In its 1932 campaign efforts, the League appears to have been mainly interested in attacking the major parties and publicizing its own platform.[47] Yet LIPA's support for its endorsees was not insubstantial. Howard Y. Williams asserted that the League's 10,000 dues-paying members were responsible for a large part of the Socialist party's financial and publicity resources. For example, LIPA members gave some 500 speeches on behalf of Norman Thomas. One historian of the Socialist party has concluded that independent "intellectuals gave more support to Thomas in 1932 than did labor."[48] Efforts were also made to lend effective support to the League's Democratic, Republican, and Socialist endorsees on the state and local levels. The endeavors in support of Norman Thomas went for naught. With the tabulation of the votes, it was quite apparent that nationally the two major parties were still very much alive. Norman Thomas polled 884,781 ballots, slightly over 2 per cent of the total vote for President. In fact, all the active third parties attracted only about 3 per cent of the ballots. Franklin D. Roosevelt had won a smashing victory in the race for dissident support.

The League for Independent Political Action refused to be crushed by the advent of the Democratic Messiah. It continued to push its double-headed program of applying pressure upon the government for social betterment and attempting to form a political party which would renounce government "for the benefit of a few." The League's adherents were assured that progressives voted for Roosevelt rather than Norman Thomas for fear that Hoover would have been re-elected if a heavy vote had been cast for the Socialist. John Dewey interpreted the election results as "a vote for a new realignment in political measures if not for it in political parties." Dewey contended that the Western agrarians had rejected the Republican party for its failure to solve the nation's economic problems and that they stood ready to repudiate the Democratic party if it also failed. "It will fail," declared the LIPA chairman. "Somebody must see to it that four years from now they do not simply swing back into the Republican party which will then be the 'promising' party."[49]

In evaluating the over-all political situation, LIPA felt that the chances for an effective new party in the coming four years were excellent. Roosevelt's election was viewed as weakening reactionary control of the government. The League gloried in the election of four new Minnesota Farmer-Labor Congressmen, and especially in the statements of Farmer-Labor leaders that their party must grow nationally. LIPA took pride in the election of Elbert Thomas of Utah and Marion Zionchek of Washington, respectively, to the Senate and House of Representatives. Thomas and Zionchek were League leaders.[50] Encouragement for the League's future activities was derived from other developments in 1932. The United Textile Workers and the American Federation of Hosiery Workers had passed convention resolutions advocating the establishment of an independent party of labor. Even the conservative president of the American Federation of Labor, William Green, had warned that the A. F. of L. would form "an in-

dependent political organization" to serve the workers' interests if necessary.[51] Farm organizations also
showed signs of increasing dissatisfaction with the
major parties. Agrarian leaders, especially in the
National Farmers' Union, were enraged when a
Democratic-Republican coalition in Congress defeated proposed unemployment relief legislation.[52]
During the summer and fall, the National Farmers'
Holiday Association, primarily a Midwestern organization, gained national attention by applying boycott
and picketing methods to force prices to equal the
cost of production. LIPA asserted that these agrarians were determined "to have relief either by ballots or by violence."[53]

In response to these developments, a switch of
emphasis was under way within LIPA. Intellectual-
ism was to be forced to take a back seat, and less stress
was to be placed upon using the Socialist party as
one of the chief vehicles for the rise of a new comprehensive party of protest. The League's officials
were to look more for support toward the membership of agrarian and working-class groups in general
and the Minnesota Farmer-Labor party in particu-
lar. While the Socialists were not to be ignored,
LIPA had been disappointed with the showing
made by them in the 1932 elections. The League, in
looking at itself, recognized that it had not become
the force in American political life which it wanted
to be. But at least it now had experience as well as
intellect, and the future looked favorable for the
formation of a broadly conceived liberal-radical

party. The League for Independent Political Action convinced itself in the bleak winter of 1932 that it had just begun its work.

Chapter II
WHO WANTS TO BE A TAIL TO THE
ROOSEVELT KITE?

When Franklin D. Roosevelt was inaugurated as President on March 4, 1933, the effects of depression had reached high tide. In February and March, industrial employment, stock market averages, and pay rolls had slumped to their all-depression floor levels, as had all agricultural and industrial wholesale prices. Bank failures had already assumed record-breaking proportions, bank holidays being declared in twenty-three states by March 3. By the time of the inauguration, the old and new officials of the Treasury had persuaded the other twenty-five states to proclaim bank holidays in an attempt to forestall further runs on deposits. Roosevelt's inaugural address was a brief but dramatic promise of action. As soon as the ceremonies were over, the new Chief Executive and his assistants applied themselves to fulfilling the pledge of a "new deal" for the American people. Congress was called into special session to give sweeping emergency powers to the Executive. The Emergency Banking Act increased credit for banks and generally strengthened their resources. The Civilian Conservation Corps, the Public Works Administration, and the Federal Emergency Relief Administration were established to furnish direct aid to the jobless. The Agricultural Adjustment Administration was authorized to refurbish agricultural buying power, while the Farm Credit Act supplied

28

a measure of rural credit and mortgage-refinancing. In an endeavor to stimulate business purchasing power and to stabilize production, the wages and hours of non-farm laborers were regulated through the National Industrial Recovery Act. These measures, of course, represented only a few of the efforts of the new administration to cope with the economic calamity that had befallen the nation.

Business soon responded favorably to the new government's efforts to resuscitate the economy. Stocks began to reflect the confidence radiating from Washington; banking was able to rise to its feet, although feebly; industrial employment and wages increased sharply, as did the wholesale prices of agricultural and industrial commodities. On the whole, agriculture, business, and labor lauded the forthright action of the government. A statement made by Henry I. Harriman, president of the United States Chamber of Commerce, in the middle of May, 1933, reflected their collective attitude: "Never in the history of the nation has an Administration more courageously and fairly attempted to deal with so many and such far-reaching problems."[1]

Although by May, many of the rank-and-file members of the League for Independent Political Action felt that perhaps Roosevelt would bring about the changes they desired, the organization's leadership maintained a skeptical attitude toward the New Deal. LIPA's leaders warned their adherents to "keep this issue clear, now and always. . . . [Roosevelt] stands for correcting some of the evils of

29

our present system. He does not stand for correcting the system itself."[2] Paul H. Douglas, writing in one of the semiofficial organs of the League, urged liberals to continue to organize and to promote their programs "so that Roosevelt may be supported when he is on the right side, so that there may be a strong group to go on where he falls short, and finally so that there may be an alternative to fascism if he fails."[3]

LIPA called for a conference, June 9-11, 1933, of political independents to start the machinery for a new party. In early May, however, a "Continental Congress" of workers and farmers met to decide upon principles for common economic and political action by the discontented and left-wing elements of the nation. LIPA, along with the Farm Holiday Association, the Conference for Progressive Labor Action, the needle trades unions, the Socialist party, and remnants of the Nonpartisan League, participated. Although the Continental Congress was dominated by the Socialists, a permanent committee was set up to facilitate and to co-ordinate liberal independent political action on state and local levels. LIPA was openly dissatisfied with what it regarded as dogmatic Socialist control of the Continental Congress, but decided to go along with the new movement for the present. The League was well aware that "disunity and factionalism mean failure. Unity spells the achievement of the cooperative commonwealth." LIPA's leaders hoped that the drawbacks of the Congress would be disposed of in a sane and demo-

cratic manner in view of the fact that the "time is
short. Chaos and fascism lie around the corner." Consequently, the League canceled its scheduled June
meeting to demonstrate its co-operative spirit.[4]

Meanwhile, the farm strike movement in the
Midwest showed signs of revival. Just a month before Roosevelt's inauguration, Milo Reno, the head
of the Farm Holiday Association, had demanded that
the new government afford immediate agricultural
relief or else a national farm strike would be initi-
ated. The potency of Reno's threat was vouched for
in the country's major newspapers and magazines.
Scattered farmyard and courthouse-step rebellions
by the Holidayers in the winter of 1932-1933 had
virtually effected an informal foreclosure moratorium from the Rocky Mountains to the Appala-
chians. Creditors were urged by state officials to
"wait awhile," and many judges were quite frankly
advising lawyers for safety's sake not to handle foreclosure cases.[5] The capitols of a number of Midwestern states were besieged by thousands of farmers,
bearing petitions signed by tens of thousands of
their comrades.

About a week after the New Deal administration
commenced, the national convention of the Farm
Holiday Association met in Des Moines to make
known its specific demands upon the government.
Delegates from sixteen states, claiming to represent
over one million farmers, called upon Congress to
enact a national moratorium on foreclosures, low-
cost debt-refinancing, federal operation of banks,

31

and a "soak-the-rich" income tax. To strengthen
their hand, the Holidayers also demanded an equit-
able bonus for veterans and relief for laborers and
city-dwellers. Congress was given until May 3 to act
upon the proposals. If it refused to comply with this
ultimatum, the Farm Holiday Association would prepare for a national farm strike. May 3 passed without
any action by the federal government. The following
day the Holidayers set May 13 as the beginning of
the strike. All agricultural commodities were to be
included in the strike, although the Association offered to establish food exchanges for the purpose of
bartering with labor groups.[6]

Prior to the date set for the commencement of the
farm strike, state and local governments worked vigorously to avert it. Insurance and mortgage companies were urged to be lenient. Governor William
Langer of North Dakota used state militia to prevent
sheriffs from making foreclosures. In Iowa, the property tax was reduced by 20 per cent, the period of
grace for tax bills was extended, and moratoria on
property were declared. Home and farm moratoria
were proclaimed in Minnesota for two years, direct
taxes on property were reduced, drastic regulations
of banks and insurance companies were introduced,
and rural public works projects were increased. In
South Dakota also there were property tax reductions and the extension of the grace period for tax
payments. Price-fixing was imposed on dairy
products in Wisconsin, while farmers were allowed
three years to redeem their defaulted property. The

day before the Farm Holiday Association was to
launch its strike, President Roosevelt signed the
hurriedly passed Agricultural Adjustment Act and
related farm-relief laws, which included provisions
for farm debt-refinancing, as well as stipulations designed to raise agricultural commodity prices. The
President also asked the farmers to cease their agitation until they could judge how their welfare would
be affected by the new measures. In response to this
request and to pressure from state officials, Milo
Reno canceled the strike call. The Farm Holiday Association leaders warned, however, that the crisis was
not over. They made it clear that this was but a
truce.[7]

Only a few local farm holidays occurred during
the summer of 1933, but the agricultural situation in
the Midwest began to tighten up in the early fall.
Wheat and livestock prices dropped in the late summer after a brief climb, and the cost of industrially
produced commodities increased. Consequently, the
Farm Holiday Association again decided to resort to
the threat of a general farm strike. The organization
called a holiday to begin October 21. The federal
government now took the position that it was up to
the governors of the Midwestern states to cope with
the situation, and many of these officials once more
did what they could to avert the strike. They felt,
however, that their tools of statecraft had generally
been exhausted in dealing with the previous May
strike threat. They were unwilling to go much further down the road to what some critics called "so-

cialized agriculture" without greater efforts being
made by the federal government. Many of the governors demanded that the national government,
through price-fixing and inflation formulae, do more
to aid the nation's farmers.[8]

In regard to this new crisis, John A. Simpson, the
respected chief of the National Farmers' Union and
one of Roosevelt's key supporters in the 1932 election, lashed out at the President in unrestrained
style. Ridiculing the solutions of the nation's problems offered by the new administration, Simpson
stated that it was hard to believe that anyone was so
ignorant as to think we could drink ourselves prosperous, borrow ourselves prosperous, or gain prosperity by the destruction of property. He advised
Roosevelt that a new deal for farmers could be
achieved overnight by executive action ordering remonetization of silver, devaluation of the gold dollar, and payment of all due public debts with legal-
tender currency. The agricultural leader warned
that either this must be accomplished or there
would be a general collapse of economic and governmental functions.[9] Governor Floyd B. Olson of
Minnesota asserted that dangerous political possibilities might develop from the continued disgruntlement of the country's workers and farmers. The
Farmer-Laborite official declared that, in Minnesota,
unless true relief for farmers was provided, "the
sound of marching feet . . . will not be strange." He
exhorted the government that "it is time for action,
not experiment. Relief to industry is not sufficient to

increase the buying power of the farmer."[10] Many labor leaders also gave vent to their feelings regarding the plight of agriculture in the Midwest. Representative of such sentiment was the declaration of the Nebraska Federation of Labor that it was behind the farm strike "100%." The executive committee of the Socialist party adopted a resolution of sincere sympathy for the strike.

The strike came off as scheduled, with not a few acts of violence: slayings, bombings, pitched battles between the farmers and police, the spreading of glass and nails on public highways, sabotage and dumping of the products of non-strikers, highway and railway blockades designed to aid searches for "illicit" produce, and bridges burned to prevent the transportation of agricultural commodities. The head of the Holidayers, Milo Reno, felt that such acts were regrettable, but added, "It's easy to counsel respect for law and order by those who are not in dire distress. It's quite another matter, however, to the farmer who sees the earnings and accumulations of a lifetime being taken away from him and his righteous requests ignored."[11]

After two weeks of the strike, the federal government decided to take positive action. Secretary of Agriculture Henry Wallace and National Recovery Administrator Hugh Johnson were dispatched to the Midwest on extensive speaking tours designed to deflate the strike movement. Their mission was to show what progress was being made to revive the nation's economy, and how propitious the future was for the country's agricultural producers. To support these tours, the government increased efforts to appease the farmers in a more concrete way. The loan program of the New Deal was stepped up, and the corn-hog production control program was put into effect in the Middle West. Actual cash benefits were received in the area early in December and served to administer the *coup de grace* to the farm strike.[12]

Although dissuaded from direct economic action, many farmers talked of third-party political action. Farm-strike leaders like Milo Reno and John Bosch were in contact with new-party advocates. It was not unusual to liken the action of the New Deal to that of an anesthesia. A remedy was demanded, not a pain-killer. Illustrative of the opinion of radical farm spokesmen were the editorial remarks of the newspaper of the Wisconsin Co-operative Milk Pool: "Farmer and city worker must combine. They are both directly injured by such a condition [inequitable economic return]. Clean out the politicians that permit such things to go on. Write laws that will correct the situation."[13] The desire for farmer-labor political action was still alive and still a threat to old-party politics.

The position of the League for Independent Political Action at this time was to wait for the New Deal to show that it could not cope effectively with the woes of the country. "If the Democratic party muffs the ball and fails to pass adequate legislation, we shall consider the whole question of a new political alignment and the advisability of calling a

National Convention in the Fall to put a united third party in the field, looking forward to capturing as many Congressional Districts as possible in 1934 and present a united front in 1936."[14] During the summer of 1933, LIPA co-operated with the Socialist-dominated Continental Congress in the sponsorship of state conventions for united liberal political and economic action in at least Michigan, Ohio, Massachusetts, Maryland, and Connecticut. By July, however, the League was ready to go ahead on its own. It feared that, if the Continental Congress' plans were followed, the nation's liberals would be politically unprepared to vie for power should the American government begin to collapse. Therefore, a conference of farm and labor leaders was called by the League for September, 1933, to stimulate formation of a new party. The Continental Congress was not repudiated but rather was "assigned" superintendency over the economic preparation of liberals for the calamity that the League was convinced would overtake the nation. LIPA's convention call reveals its anxiety: "Even as we go to press there are signs that a collapse may be right ahead. . . . *We are living on top of a volcano.* If we are not prepared we will go to smash as Rome and former civilizations went to smash."[15] League leaders made it clear that they did not want to become left-wing sympathizers with the New Deal. A more radical policy was called for to attract the discontented of the nation. The ultimate aim of LIPA was described as being the establishment of a "Co-operative

Commonwealth, with a scientifically planned economic system, based on social control of the means of production."[16]

The LIPA convention held in Chicago on September 2 and 3 attracted mainly agrarian elements. Selden Rodman, reporting it in the *New Republic*, wrote that "such conventions have met before. Many of the delegates were hardened convention-trotters. As the meeting opened they yawned. There was a perfect hurricane of speeches. Liberals talked and scolded. Radicals expostulated and shook their fingers. Farmers gave ominous reports of the N.R.A. and of their impending strike. General Coxey sat in the back of the hall and silently passed out his familiar leaflets. One man even got up and defended the capitalist system. There were bedlam, confusion, personal bitterness." All those invited to this affair agreed, however, that something had to be done to salvage the nation's future; all were searching vigorously for a plan, and many had found fairly similar programs for bringing the country to the Co-operative Commonwealth; all wondered, though, where they might find a leader capable of arousing and inspiring the American people? Then ex-Congressman Thomas R. Amlie of Wisconsin spoke to the group, and it was felt that the country's new-party advocates had found their man. Using an impressive array of facts and logic, this youthful and dynamic former Nonpartisan League organizer proclaimed the depression to be the herald of the final collapse of capitalistic institutions in this country. Amlie asserted that there could be only one answer to the situation: the formation of a people's party, one that was anti-wealth, anti-capitalism, and anti-big business.[17]

The enthusiastic delegates had to be restrained from immediately launching a new party, in large part because the plaform they adopted was not regarded as being satisfactory for political action. In size and detail, it certainly was puny and lacking in ingenuity compared with the program presented by LIPA the previous year. It called for a well-paid job for every workingman and security of land tenure for farmers. All men were to be protected against the hazards of life by a governmental system of insurance against unemployment, illness, accidents, and old age. Maternity insurance and educational and infancy allowances were to be paid to give financial stability to the family. To protect consumers, the conference demanded the abolition of speculation in the necessities of life, and public ownership of natural resources, railways, utilities, mines, and other basic industries. Also proposed were governmental monopolization of foreign trade, nationalization of banking, credit, and currency, and cash payment of the soldiers' bonus. All this was to be financed by the proceeds from "heavy taxes" on "unearned wealth."[18]

Instead of forming a new national party, the Chicago convention was persuaded to establish the Farmer-Labor Political Federation. This was viewed as the instrument through which farmers, laborers, and intellectuals could work for the formation of state third-party tickets in 1934. John Dewey was made honorary chairman of the new organization, Amlie and Howard Y. Williams chairman and national organizer, respectively, and Alfred M. Bingham, the editor of *Common Sense,* executive secretary. The Farmer-Labor Political Federation set a deadline of a year for itself, and promised significant organizational results in that time. It was announced that LIPA would not merge with FLPF until later; as the latter's twin, the League would serve to appeal to groups that might be suspicious of the Farmer-Labor label.[19] The September, 1933, conference was hailed by *Common Sense* as "a real achievement"; FLPF had successfully enticed the truly liberal leaders of Midwestern agriculture and labor into the third-party fold. These sons of the Middle Border, *Common Sense* felt, went to a no-strings-attached conference and convinced themselves of the truth of what LIPA had been preaching for years.[20] Unfortunately, many prominent LIPA members were not members of the new organization; they had reset their courses along New Deal or Socialist lines. Conspicuously absent was the editor of the *Nation,* Oswald Garrison Villard. Villard, who had been the treasurer of LIPA (and one of its chief financial supporters), refused a similar post with FLPF. Later, he recommended that political independents should endeavor to strengthen Roosevelt's hand.[21]

The League for Independent Political Action and the Farmer-Labor Political Federation stepped

40

up action in the months following the Chicago convention. They made their attacks upon both the
right and the left. The general withdrawal of Socialists from LIPA activities was decried. Calling for
unity among radicals, LIPA declared that only sincere compromise and flexibility in aims and tactics
could achieve real advancement toward a democratically controlled economy and government. The
League asserted, however, that it was ready to co-
operate with the Socialist party and to aid in keeping
the doors of FLPF open to Socialists. In late 1933,
LIPA sponsored a series of radio programs over the
National Broadcasting Company designed to show
the people what they could accomplish with democratic social planning. This educational series fea-
tured talks by scholars such as George S. Counts, Paul
Douglas, Harold Rugg, and Henry Pratt Fairchild.[22]
Forums were sponsored by FLPF at which top-level
union and farm leaders discussed their problems, the
state of the union, and political action. One of the
more successful of these meetings, held in New York
City early in 1934, was addressed by A. F. Whitney,
president of the Brotherhood of Railway Trainmen,
Milo Reno, chief of the Farm Holiday Association,
and Thomas R. Amlie. Whitney condemned the
present management of the nation's railways and
called for their nationalization. He tagged the National Recovery Administration the "last vestige of
hope for the capitalist system," but declared that it
had failed to aid farmers and railway workers, and to
bring "conditions people had a right to expect." The

union leader warned, however, that labor would remain nonpartisan until the liberal third-party advocates formed a united political organization and agreed upon a satisfactory program. Reno called the New Deal an outright failure. He could see only one road out of the swamp of economic instability—the unification of all workers and producers in a third party. Amlie then proceeded to point to the "clear" need for a new party. He also presented a petition for a constitutional convention, which stated that the present Constitution prevents essential changes. The petition called for restriction of the powers of the Supreme Court and provisions for the government to be allowed to nationalize industries. Reno felt that this should be deferred until a people's government had tried to do everything possible under the Constitution to achieve a sound and fair economic system.[23]

FLPF and LIPA excoriated the New Deal at every turn, calling attention to what they felt were the inadequacies of the administration's programs. In "An Open Letter to President Roosevelt," *Common Sense* declared that "you have in your own acts and speeches . . . shown some realization that the old days of *laissez faire* capitalism were over, but you have vainly hoped that a controlled capitalism might be possible, and the result has been more monopoly than ever." The magazine conceded that Roosevelt had relieved some of the suffering of the unemployed. It asserted, however, that not only had insufficient funds been allocated to public-works agencies, but that, except for the Tennessee Valley Authority, they had scrupulously avoided producing low-cost commodities for the needy. The New Deal was indicted for failing even to attempt enactment of an unemployment insurance or a social-security system. The Reconstruction Finance Corporation and the National Recovery Administration were seen as doing far more for business interests than for the really needy of the land. Concerning the agricultural situation, the magazine remarked that "a billion dollars in bribes to farmers to pacify their resentment, and get them to cut down production while many are hungry, is not the way out." Roosevelt was accused of "money juggling" instead of facing the dire need for a sound national monetary and credit system. Speculation and profiteering had gone untouched, *Common Sense* claimed, while a fair graduated income tax had been forsaken for "patching up some of the holes in our income tax laws." The President was condemned because he had "sponsored a bigger army and navy and allowed us to enter a world armaments race," and he was held to be not bold enough to attempt to stop the march of the world toward war. On the other hand, the Chief Executive was congratulated for extending diplomatic recognition to the Soviet Union and for allowing the war-debt problem "to die a natural death." He received another compliment for avoiding the "insoluble mess" in the Far East.[24] Six months later, the New Deal was judged even more harshly by *Common Sense:* "Failure is a hard word. It is too early to convince Roosevelt's supporters that he is a failure. Yet we believe the record indicates that nothing but failure can be expected from the New Deal."[25]

The Farmer-Labor Political Federation was, however, doing more than just editorializing its opposition to the New Deal. It was devoting more and more organizational energy to exploiting discontent. Within three months after its establishment, FLPF reported organizational activities and memberships in twenty-six states.[26] It increased contacts with disgruntled liberals, farm and labor leaders, especially concentrating on the Midwest, where dissent seemed to be strongest. The formation of the Iowa Farmer-Labor party was successfully encouraged, although the organization itself failed to gain significant strength. The South Dakota Farmer-Labor Economic Federation was created to capture the Democratic party and, failing that, to form a new state party. But among the most important of FLPF endeavors was its role in the establishment of the Wisconsin Progressive party.[27]

The League for Independent Political Action had been trying to develop sentiment for a new party in Wisconsin since 1929, and the Farmer-Labor Political Federation, led by Amlie, invaded the state to redouble these efforts.[28] FLPF looked to Wisconsin's Progressive Republican faction, nominally led by Senator Robert M. La Follette, Jr., as the core of new-party activities. Having lost control of the Republican party and the state with the rush of many of their supporters to the Roosevelt bandwagon, the Progressive Republicans now found that they were

44

for the first time since 1900 virtually powerless. FLPF organizers attempted to make it clear to Progressive Republicans that something had to be done immediately if progressive principles were to continue to be of significance in Wisconsin. It was pointed out that the currently impotent Republican party could no longer be used as a convenient political haven. On the other hand, it was obvious that local Democrats were not following Roosevelt's suggestion that they share their spoils with the President's Progressive supporters. Many Progressives, spurred on by the FLPF organizers, concluded that their faction could only hope to mend its fortunes in the role of an independent political party.

The FLPF organizers were to be aided in their campaign for the formation of a new Wisconsin party by the unimpressive record of the Democratic Governor, Albert Schmedeman, and the legislature's conservative temper. Moreover, during 1933 and 1934, Wisconsin's grain and livestock producers were to be severely affected by relatively high local taxes and increasingly sharper competition with Western agriculture. This group of farmers constituted one of the more active groups within the state's farm holiday movement. In addition, Wisconsin, the center of the country's dairy industry, had been seriously hit by a special crisis on the milk market. Price wars between milk retailers in 1933 forced the already drastically diminished income of dairy farmers to dip even lower. Little relief was offered by the Agricultural Adjustment Act, which, for the most part, did not extend to them.[29] Combined with the inability of the state government to ameliorate the results of the price wars, this situation prompted a series of milk strikes led by the powerful Wisconsin Co-operative Milk Pool.

In addition to agricultural troubles, Wisconsin was beset by a wave of labor strikes. The usual answer of the state to these, as well as the farm strikes, was force. For example, 200 pickets and spectators—including the president of the Wisconsin State Federation of Labor, Henry Ohl, Jr.—were gassed, and some of them were beaten when city and county law enforcement officers in Milwaukee broke the picket line at the Garton Toy Company.[30] For twenty days in the summer of 1934, Governor Schmedeman had the National Guard encamped in the industrial town of Kohler to quell labor unrest. The continuance of officially approved farm fore-closures and the crude action of the Schmedeman government in coping with farm and labor strikes gave organized agriculture and labor little reason to be satisfied with Wisconsin's Democratic administration. By the spring of 1934, it took but little urging from FLPF organizers to stimulate the State Federation of Labor, the Co-operative Milk Pool, and the Wisconsin Farm Holiday Association to call for the emergence of a state farmer-labor party.[31]

FLPF, of course, utilized the increasing new-party sentiment among farmers and workers to bring pressure on Progressive Republican leaders to form an independent state party. Although Senator La

46

Follette was opposed to taking the Progressives out of the Republican party, his brother, a former governor of Wisconsin, showed some interest. Even Philip La Follette, however, refrained from identifying himself with the new movement until it showed signs of succeeding.[32] By the beginning of 1934, it was apparent that new-party sentiment dominated the rank-and-file of Wisconsin Progressive Republicans. Facing an election contest in 1934, Senator La Follette decided that he could only tread the path pointed out by his "followers." Therefore, in a convention held at Fond du Lac, May 19, to consider the formation of an independent progressive party, the Senator and most of the recalcitrants indicated that they were ready to go along with the new-party supporters. The Senator rationalized his decision on the grounds that the Democratic party was in the process of becoming controlled by "the same reactionary interests that dominate the Republican party." The Fond du Lac convention enthusiastically voted, 252 to 44, to form a new party—the Wisconsin Progressive party.[33]

The newly achieved political independence was reflected in the party's 1934 platform. Herein, the party issued a forthright denunciation of the existing American economic system. The Progressives contended that since the "cruelty and stupidity" of our economic system had resulted in "widespread and continued poverty and insecurity," it was imperative "to build a new order of security and plenty for America." More specifically, the Progressives pro-

47

posed that the powers of government be used to re-
finance farm and home mortgages at low interest
rates, to defer foreclosures on farms and homes, to
institute a series of internal-improvement projects,
and to pay the long-delayed bonus to World War I
veterans. The Progressives held that measures such
as these would rescue the nation from the abyss of
depression by increasing purchasing power, by halt-
ing the trend toward the concentration of wealth,
and by restoring the people's confidence in themselves. Moreover, they urged financial security for
all, through the enactment of a universal old-age
pension, unemployment insurance, accident insurance, and minimum-wage and hour laws. They also
felt that recurrence of the inflation of the 1920's and
of the subsequent depression could be prevented. To
this end, the Progressives demanded the reduction
and stabilization of consumer-producer price differ-
entials, government operation of industries where
price competition was not practiced, government encouragement of consumers' and producers' co-operatives, a more sharply graduated income tax, and
levying of taxes on securities and dividends. The
Progressives promised to give a bigger share in the
affairs of state to more people by seeking universal
adoption of the initiative and the referendum. Since
war was one of the major causes of the decay of political and economic democracy, the Constitution of
the United States should be amended to require that
any proposed declaration of war should be submitted to a popular referendum, except when the

nation was attacked by military force. They also announced that they stood ready to increase state services like soil conservation and inexpensive higher education for all.[34] Shorn of identification with either of the two major parties, the Progressives felt that they would now be able—on the basis of their program—to attract erstwhile colleagues and disgruntled New Dealers and Socialists into their camp.

Unfortunately for the Farmer-Labor Political Federation, Thomas Amlie and his cohorts were not numerically strong enough to control the high councils of the new party. The La Follette brothers were able successfully to assert their hereditary claim to leadership and set the course of the Progressive party along less idealistic political lines. The La Follettes saw that the surge of Progressive energy resulting from the new-party experiment would enable them to force political horse-trades with President Roosevelt. It is interesting to note that presidential support for Senator La Follette's 1934 re-election campaign came only after the Progressive party had been admitted to the Wisconsin ballot by popular demand. Moreover, after the 1934 elections, Roosevelt and the La Follettes agreed informally that the conservative Wisconsin Democratic party would be kept weak politically if the Progressives would give support to the liberal features of the New Deal program. This plan was implemented by giving the Progressives control of many choice federal offices in Wisconsin, including the state Works Progress Administration.[35]

Yet it should not be assumed that the new-national-party ideas of the FLPF organizers were lost upon the Progressives. The party's 1934 platform declared that "Progressives in Wisconsin, cutting loose from all connections with the two old reactionary parties in this crisis, have founded a new national party." This document illustrates further the national political ambitions of the Progressives in that only eleven of the forty-three planks were exclusively state or local in character.[36] Most of the Wisconsin Progressives were persuaded that their party would eventually merge with other liberal and leftist forces to form an effective national party, even if it was to be only a New Deal party as distinguished from the Democratic party. They were motivated in this conclusion not only by altruistic or idealistic factors, but also by reasons of a sound political nature. They were aware that political operations restricted to a single state could not long appeal successfully to adherents who had to choose among Democratic, Republican, or Socialist candidates for President. Many Progressive leaders were further convinced that should one of the major parties bring about national economic recovery, they would, as a local third party, be without bargaining power in making a transition into the ranks of either the Democratic or Republican party.

Looking at the opinion of radicals and liberals, we find a mixed reaction regarding the new party. Of course, the liberals and leftists of FLPF persuasion were far from satisfied with the Wisconsin Progressive party. Referring to the Fond du Lac meeting, Thomas Amlie wrote that "the general feeling is . . . the organized farmers and organized workers were betrayed at the conference. They went expecting a radical party to be organized. They got, instead, some more old-time La Follette Progressivism." Amlie and Howard Y. Williams made it quite clear that they would strive for FLPF control of the Wisconsin Progressive party so that it could be more expressive of its radical and farmer-laborite elements.[37] The results of this activity will be discussed later on. The Socialist party newspaper in Wisconsin, the *Milwaukee Leader,* referred to the Fond du Lac meeting as a "steam roller" convention and pronounced the new party to "be a tail to the Roosevelt kite." The Socialists were quite visibly disturbed by Philip La Follette's warning that the Wisconsin Progressive party could not be a class party. The *Milwaukee Leader* agreed with the observations of many labor leaders that the new organization was simply "a personal party for the old La Follette machine."[38] Although the Wisconsin Socialists were not yet ready to merge their fortunes with the Progressives, they could not help concluding that their enemies were not the Progressives, but the capitalists. Common sense led them to realize that Socialist and Progressive legislators would in the main cooperate in the state legislature.[39] In Minnesota, Farmer-Labor leader Henry Teigan lauded the formation of the Wisconsin Progressive party, saying that it "omens well for the organization of a national

third party in 1936." Senator Lynn J. Frazier of
North Dakota, a liberal Republican, was of the
opinion that "a third party in America is not only
necessary, it is inevitable, if the Republican and
Democratic parties continue to be dominated by
reactionaries." Fiorello LaGuardia hailed the new
party with similar comments.[40]

Soon after the adjournment of the Fond du Lac
conference, local Progressive workers set out to pro-
cure the signatures needed to put the new party on
the Wisconsin ballot. Within a month, over 120,000
Wisconsin citizens—twelve times the number required—had petitioned the state government to give
the Progressive party ballot privileges.[41] Encouraged
by this impressive showing, the Progressives went
into battle. Robert La Follette, Jr., ran for re-election
to the Senate, and Philip La Follette sought to regain the governorship. In the general elections, the
La Follette brothers and the Progressive candidate
for secretary of state triumphed over their old-party
rivals. The party's nominees for the three other state-
wide offices lost by less than 2 per cent of the total
vote cast in each case. Progressive candidates also
won forty-five seats in the state assembly, while the
Democrats held thirty-five, the Republicans seventeen, and the Socialists three. The new state senate
was to contain fourteen Democrats, thirteen Progressives, and six Republicans. Progressives—including
Thomas R. Amlie and George J. Schneider, Farmer-
Labor Political Federation leaders—were elected to

seven of Wisconsin's ten seats in the United States House of Representatives.[42]

In an editorial on the election, the Democratic state chairman, Charles Broughton, commented bitterly that "the friendly attitude of the national administration toward Senator La Follette made him an outstanding figure in the election yesterday, and as a result brought victory to his brother, Philip F. La Follette."[43] The *Janesville Daily Gazette,* a prominent unofficial Republican newspaper, declared that the election results meant that the Progressives and their adherents "will be regimented in favor of a new [national] party to be heard from in other states and perhaps, if it grows enough, will be conjured with in 1936. It will at least be powerful enough to form a threat to Democratic success."[44] The *Gazette* held the election of Progressive Congressman Amlie to be a sign—and not a happy one— of this possibility.[45] In any event, the Wisconsin Progressive party had proved that it had grass roots strength. Not only did it appreciably diminish the power of the two traditional parties in Wisconsin, but it found itself in a position where it practically controlled the state government. The Progressive success also marked a victory—although a qualified one—for the advocates of a national liberal-leftist party. Even the reluctant Senator La Follette declared that he was in the new party to stay, and he predicted the establishment of a new-national-party line-up.[46]

Meanwhile, the strategy of committing the Minnesota Farmer-Labor party to the goals of the Farmer-Labor Political Federation was in the process of development. Howard Y. Williams was the leader of FLPF activities in Minnesota. His goal was to convince the majority of Farmer-Laborites that the depression could be stopped only by the passing of measures more bold and radical than those adopted by the New Deal. Once this was done, he hoped that the Minnesota Farmer-Labor party would stop cooperating with the Democrats and would assume leadership, possibly along with the Wisconsin Progressives, of the drive for a new national third party. All the ordinary methods of persuasion were used, including conferences with Farmer-Labor leaders, speeches, the sending out of pamphlets and letters, and effective use of the publications and meetings of the party. These activities were apparently progressing only slowly toward success. It was decided, therefore, that something quick and startling, that would receive wide publicity, was in order. What better instrument could be used, concluded the third-party supporters, than the official 1934 Minnesota Farmer-Labor platform, fashioned into a document that would show the need for decidedly more radical political and governmental action?

By the time of the party's biennial convention in St. Paul late in March, 1934, a zealous minority of delegates had been organized to buttonhole in support of the FLPF goals. Williams had secured appointment as chairman of the convention's platform committee, and several of his colleagues had been strategically placed as program speakers to whip up sentiment for the adoption of a radical platform.[47] Wittingly or not, Farmer-Labor Governor Floyd Olson also helped to develop the convention's enthusiasm for a radical platform: "Now I am frank to say that I am not a liberal. I enjoy working on a common basis with liberals for their platforms, etc., but I am not a liberal. I am what I want to be—I am a radical. I am a radical in the sense that I want a definite change in the system. I am not satisfied with tinkering, I am not satisfied with patching, I am not satisfied with hanging a laurel wreath on burglars and thieves and pirates and calling them code authorities or something else. I am not satisfied with that. . . . What is the ultimate we are seeking? . . . The ultimate is a Cooperative Commonwealth."[48] Certainly, no more powerful support for the goals of the FLPF forces in the convention could have been found than in the radical statement of the chieftain of the Minnesota Farmer-Labor party.

After fighting a bitter but successful battle in the platform committee, Williams and his friends presented their spirited version of "a real farmer-labor platform." The stirring exhortations of the radical, new-party supporters soon enveloped the convention in a flame of almost revolutionary speeches and manifestoes. "All distinctions between moderates and radicals had momentarily disappeared in a fit of wild crusading ardor." The Williams platform was vigorously endorsed by the convention during the early morning hours of March 29.[49] The preamble to the platform gives some idea of its radical nature:

> Only a complete reorganization of our social structure into a cooperative commonwealth will bring economic security and prevent a prolonged period of further suffering among the people.
>
> We, therefore, declare that capitalism has failed and immediate steps must be taken by the people to abolish capitalism in a peaceful and lawful manner and that a new sane and just society must be established; a system where all the natural resources, machinery of production, transportation and communication shall be owned by the government and operated democratically for the benefit of the people and not for the benefit of the few.

More specifically, the document called for state aid to co-operative marketing and purchasing agencies; ultimate public ownership of mines, water power, transportation and communication, banks, packing plants, factories, and all public utilities except those owned by co-operatives; state regulation of labor's hours and wages; non-profit state life insurance and insurance for unemployment, accidents, sickness, maternity, old age, fire, cyclone, and hail; state publication of textbooks and free distribution to students; termination of compulsory military training in state institutions; repeal of tax exemption on securities; increased taxes on large incomes and inheritances; and creation of a state central bank to serve as a depository for all state funds and to give loans to banks.[50]

The opposition parties almost immediately opened up a barrage of denunciation and vituperation upon what they referred to as the "Socialist platform." The *Minneapolis Journal* declared the document to be "more enlightening than pages of comments or hours of campaign speeches." This newspaper suggested that it might be well worth while for the Democrats and the Republicans to reprint the Farmer-Labor platform as a piece of campaign literature. State Senator Vin Weber, an implacable foe of Governor Olson, asserted that "for the first time . . . the Farmer Labor party goes before the voters stripped of camouflage and expediency, revealed as the menace it is, supporting principles of government un-American and unwise to experiment with." These comments on the Minnesota Farmer-Labor party's platform set the pace for the opposition oratory which was to flood every corner of Minnesota with warnings of the "Communist menace" during the ensuing election campaign.[51] The *New York Times* predicted that the adoption of the "Socialist platform" by the Minnesota Farmer-Laborites would give the Republicans or the "regular" Democrats a good chance to obtain control of the state government.[52]

When the ardor of the Farmer-Laborites cooled down they began to fear that a major political error had been committed. Large-scale defections were reported from the rural areas, and small businessmen and professional people were declared to be frightened at the prospects of the continuance of the Farmer-Labor government. Many party members were soon sharing the opinion of George Leonard, pioneer Minneapolis labor lawyer, that the platform had "resuscitated the Republican corpse." Fortunately for the drooping spirits of the party's members, Governor Olson declared uncompromising support of the platform throughout the campaign. He accused the opposition of "endeavoring to frighten the people of Minnesota so that the people will regard them as saviors, and they will again have the opportunity to loot the state in the name of salvation."[53] The party's leaders also took pains, in carefully planned statements, to "explain" what the platform meant. For example, the demand for state operation of factories was interpreted as referring only to idle industrial plants. Moreover, it was asserted that the "Farmer-Labor party is opposed to state ownership and operation of small business such as grocery stores, meat shops, department stores, millinery establishments, drug stores, and similar enterprises." These modifications had a calming effect upon the apprehensions of the state's voters, but still allowed the Minnesota Farmer-Labor party officers to say that they were not repudiating any part of the platform.[54]

Although the Farmer-Laborites lost some citizen support in the 1934 elections, they were able to retain control of the state government. Olson was reelected governor, despite the independent candidacy of veteran Nonpartisan Leaguer A. C. Townley, which tended to draw away liberal-leftist votes. Olson won by a still impressive plurality of 72,453 votes as compared to one of 188,357 in 1932. Reductions in the pluralities of other successful Farmer-Labor nominees were apparent. The party's delegation to the House of Representatives was cut from five to three; this, however, was possibly due to the change in voting for Representatives in Congress, from the "at large" to the "district" system of election. The party lost only two state-wide contests, as was true in 1932, and re-elected Henrik Shipstead to the United States Senate.[55]

Although many observers attributed the Farmer-Labor losses mainly to the 1934 "Socialist platform," it must be remembered that the excitement attendant upon the 1932 presidential campaign had roused more discontented Minnesotans to vote then than in 1934. Moreover, other troubles hampered the electoral efforts of the Farmer-Laborites. A series of truck strikes in the Twin Cities in 1934, aggravated by violence on the part of business and labor, worked to the disadvantage of the Farmer-Labor party. The party was charged with giving direct aid to the strikers, and with stimulating thoughts of revolutionary violence.[56] Quite a furor was created by the statement of the recently resigned State Commissioner of Education that the party levied a 3 per cent assessment on employees' salaries in the Department of State. Then again, the Farmer-Laborites were accused of receiving kickbacks and campaign aid from employees on federal public works projects. These charges were not denied by the state administration, and later were proved to be partially true. This, of course, damaged the universal argument of

59

liberals and leftists that once in power they would not follow the patterns of the spoils system and patronage used by the old parties.[57] In view of these extenuating factors, it is hard to conclude that the platform strategy of Howard Y. Williams was chiefly responsible for weakening the appeal of the Minnesota Farmer-Labor party to the voters. It did, however, force the Farmer-Laborites to espouse, at least technically, a more radical program, and perhaps created more sentiment among party members for the formation of a new national party.

By the end of 1934, the Farmer-Labor Political Federation had become established as an element in American left-wing politics. It was active from coast-to-coast in its own right and by virtue of having gradually absorbed the Eastern and Far Western branches of the League for Independent Political Action. FLPF had concentrated its efforts, since its birth, in the Middle West, especially in Minnesota and Wisconsin. In these two states, it had gained significant influence with the leadership and rank-and-file of the two dominant state parties. Yet the FLPF leaders realized that before a strong new party and the Co-operative Commonwealth were to become possible of achievement discontent had to ripen more and a great deal more work was necessary. The latter could be done by FLPF, but the former waited upon time.

Chapter III
TILLING THE SOIL OF
DISSATISFACTION

It seemed obvious by 1935 that despite the grandiose plans of the New Deal to revive the nation's economy, the basic problems of the depression remained largely unsolved. That the Roosevelt administration had achieved little success in its search for "Recovery" since the middle of 1934 was well supported by the facts. The depressed payrolls in manufacturing industries remained fairly stable from about April, 1934, to the fall of the following year. The prevailing trend of wholesale prices for farm products in 1935 and the first quarter of 1936 was downward. Between early 1933 and 1934, unemployment rolls had been reduced 16 per cent, but from 1934 to 1935 the number of jobless persons decreased only by about 6 per cent.[1]

The nation's lack of economic progress and other factors caused considerable ferment in labor, agrarian, and professional left-of-center political groups in late 1934 and in 1935. Labor was especially resentful of the treatment afforded the Wagner Fair Labor Practices Bill and the Connery Thirty-hour Work Week Bill. It seemed to many union leaders that the courts, the Congress, and even the President were opposed to these proposals. William Green, referring to the bills in a fighting speech before a New York City labor rally, announced that "we will refuse to work and will mobilize our entire economic strength until we get our rights." He exhorted all workers to demand the passage of these two legislative measures.[2] On May 27, 1935, when the Supreme Court invalidated both the National Industrial Recovery Act and the Frazier-Lemke Farm Mortgage Act, labor and agriculture suffered discouraging setbacks. The loss to the farmers was less severe because of state legislation providing moratoria, and the speedy action of Congress in passing new "court-proof" mortgage legislation. As for the lapsing of the labor sections of the N.I.R.A., reports of wage cuts and extensions of work hours were wholesale. Labor resisted the judicial encroachment on its recently won privileges by launching a wave of strikes.[3] Increased pressure was also applied on Congress and, consequently, the Wagner Act was passed in July. Although the statute gave labor even more protection than had been provided for under the N.I.R.A., the unions remained on an insecure footing until the law's constitutionality was adjudged two years later. After these vexing experiences with the government, many elements of organized labor looked with increasing favor upon independent political action. William Green, however, personally opposed the resolves of various AFL affiliates for the formation of a new party, believing that they represented less the opinion of workingmen than the wishes of the Kremlin. The Federation's 1935 convention approved Green's position, although it is significant that thirteen new party resolutions were offered by as many international unions and state federations as compared with only two the year before.[4]

Farmers appeared, on the surface of things, to be less dissatisfied than their brothers in the labor movement. In the spring of 1935, the wheat farmers of the nation voted 404,417 to 62,303 to continue the wheat adjustment program of the Agricultural Adjustment Administration; in the autumn, 943,982 corn-hog farmers voted six-to-one in favor of retaining their A.A.A. program.[5] Yet there were still stirrings of agrarian discontent. A large number of farmers were opposed to the A.A.A., although they participated in its activities to get their share of what they felt were its dubious benefits. The Farmers' Union groups in at least Iowa, Nebraska, Pennsylvania, and Wisconsin condemned the A.A.A., generally on the grounds that prosperity could not be derived from scarcity of agricultural products. K. W. Hones, the Wisconsin Farmers' Union president, represented the opinion of many Union members when he repudiated the two "capitalist" parties and energetically urged the adoption of the co-operative commonwealth system.[6] Even more indicative of discontent was the resolution of the some 10,000 delegates to the 1935 National Farm Holiday Association convention calling for the immediate "building of a third party" of farmers and laborers by progressive groups. The Farm Holiday Association, which maintained friendly relations with the Farmer-Labor Political Federation, was also committed to a program "of public [i.e., co-operative] ownership of public utilities, natural resources and such basic industries as are best conducted by society."[7]

Many farmers were not so much opposed to Roosevelt and his ideas as to the Democratic party. They felt that on the local level the Democrats were just as unsympathetic to the problems of farmers and laborers as were the Republicans. The *South Dakota News* complained, "We got the New Deal through the Democratic party, that is to say, we got it in the neck." This newspaper accused Governor Tom Berry of refusing to aid the state's farmers in fighting the depression, of cutting off relief through the use of political maneuvers, and of using Justice Department operatives against picket lines. Noting that "the Republican party certainly was no better," the *News* claimed that it found it impossible to support either old party. It advised that "the time has come in South Dakota to build a Farmer Labor party that will stand and fight for the things we need."[8]

Dairymen, many of them incensed at being virtually excluded from the benefits of the A.A.A., were alarmed further by the agreement reached in 1935 to reduce American tariffs on Canadian dairy products. Strongly worded but unsuccessful protests against the agreement were dispatched to Washington by leaders of the industry. During the 1936 campaign, the Republicans, including presidential candidate Alfred Landon, cited and deplored the fall in the price of cheese as a result of greatly increased imports from Canada. Regarded as a serious issue, the Republican charges brought replies not only from the Secretaries of State and Agriculture but from the President.[9] Those Progressive and Farmer-Labor politicians who represented dairy areas generally were able to stay out of this cross fire by condemning the trade agreements and then entreating the administration for relief for their constituents.

Dissatisfaction was also developing in other areas. The fear of war was not exclusively a possession of the progressives and the radicals, but they had, with some success, linked their campaign for pacifism with warnings against fascism. A good deal of their energy was devoted to winning the country's college students for action against war and fascism. These agitations led to a number of demonstrations on the campuses of the nation. For example, in April, 1935, some 60,000 college students paraded for peace and civil rights. The demonstrators displayed opposition to Roosevelt, the Reserve Officers Training Corps, Huey Long, and Father Coughlin. Counter-demonstrations by groups of "patriot" students caused riots at places like Chicago and Harvard.[10]

California politics was in ferment during the 1930's. In 1934, Upton Sinclair made his famous bid for political power. His program called for state establishment of agricultural and industrial colonies on idle property where the unemployed could support themselves and also produce for underpaid job-holders elsewhere. Under the auspices of a self-created organization known as "End Poverty in Civilization," the well-known author endeavored to become the Democratic nominee for governor of Cali-

65

fornia. President Roosevelt was apparently uncon-
cerned about Sinclair's E.P.I.C. activity, although
James Farley, the chairman of the Democratic National Committee, openly supported George Creel
for the nomination. Creel was defeated by Sinclair
in the primary election, and the novelist waged a
strong but unsuccessful battle for the governorship.[11]
In the same election, two radical third parties, the
Commonwealth and the Progressive parties, were
represented by the energetic Raymond Haight.
Haight polled over 300,000 votes, which, together
with Sinclair's votes, meant that a clear majority of
ballots were cast for radical candidates.[12]

Trouble was developing elsewhere in the Far
West. Ray McKaig, one of the chief proponents of
the new-party idea in the Pacific Northwest, described the Democratic administration of Washington state as "a flop." He noted that it had created a
good deal of dissatisfaction by opposing the trade
unions and the organized farmers of the state. He reported that in Oregon the governor had ordered the
leaders of organized agriculture to leave the state
capitol and to return to their farms where "the birds
twitter and tweet." In Idaho, where he served as an
official of the State Grange, McKaig asserted, the
Democratic leadership was inclined to be high-
handed rather than democratic.[13] The forces of discontent in the Pacific Northwest responded to the
situation described by McKaig in almost militant
fashion. Led by Senator Homer Bone and Lewis
Schwellenbach, the 200,000-member Washington

Commonwealth Federation gained virtual control of the Democratic party. In Oregon's special gubernatorial election of 1935, Peter Zimmerman, running as an independent backed by the Grange and the State Federation of Labor, garnered one third of the vote. This ferment served as the basis for the organization of the Oregon Commonwealth Federation by Zimmerman and his associates, which was to exercise significant influence within the state's Democratic party. Both the Washington and Oregon Commonwealth Federations were affiliated with the Farmer-Labor Political Federation and declared their goal to be the "Cooperative Commonwealth." In Idaho, however, Senator Borah, by appealing to liberals, was able to divert most of the dissidents into his own camp. Representative Jerry O'Connell, an FLPF member, was able to swing considerable weight on behalf of progressives and radicals in the Montana Democratic party.[14] FLPF organizers were busy between 1934 and 1936 aiding these various Western movements, which they expected would become state affiliates of a new Farmer-Labor party. Failing that, of course, they hoped that these movements would capture the Democratic party in the West for the "Cooperative Commonwealth."

One place in the nation where radical activity was virtually nonexistent was the South. Socialists and liberals had, however, given some stimulus to the organization of one Southern working-class element—the tenant farmer. The Southern Tenant Farmers' Union had been established in July, 1934,

67

in order to secure some measure of relief for the "landed proletariat." The growing membership lists of this organization, while gratifying to its Socialist and liberal sponsors, fostered a violent reaction on the part of some Southern conservatives. "Although the Union has made no demands, has called no strikes and has committed not one act of violence, hundreds of members have been evicted from the land, mobbed, beaten, illegally arrested, jailed and shot, meetings have been broken up and homes riddled with bullets." Pleas from the officers and members of the Southern Tenant Farmers' Union for the protection of their civil rights went unheeded by local, state, and federal officials. It was hoped by most left-wing leaders that this situation would explode the Southern one-party system and thereby accrue to the advantage of advocates of independent political action.[15]

Meanwhile, there was growing uneasiness among the progressive supporters of the Roosevelt administration. It was authoritatively reported that many of the progressive contact men who had secured votes for the President's 1932 candidacy were growing restive in view of increased third-party activity.[16] Interior Secretary Harold L. Ickes, in his diary, recorded the concern of the Vice President, the Attorney General, and the Secretaries of State and Commerce with the wavering of progressives in the Democratic ranks. Ickes also reported that Rexford Tugwell, the Undersecretary of Agriculture, had reluctantly concluded that Roosevelt could not possibly make any further efforts to cope with the depression effectively because he had been stymied by big business interests.[17] The growing tension between the administration and progressives was revealed in other ways. Progressive leaders were shocked by the manner in which Bronson Cutting, the progressive Republican Senator from New Mexico, was treated.[18] While Senator Cutting had given effective support to Roosevelt in 1932 and to the advanced features of the New Deal program, his campaign for re-election in 1934 was strongly opposed by the national Democratic organization. Cutting won the election, although his narrow margin of victory led the Democrats to contest his election. On his way back East from one of the subsequent hearings, the Senator was killed in an airplane crash. His erstwhile Democratic opponent, Denis Chavez, was appointed to succeed him in the Senate. As Chavez was conducted down the Senate aisle to take the oath of office, Senators Hiram Johnson, La Follette, Norris, Nye, and Shipstead departed in protest. Borah, who was absent, declared that he was with them "in spirit" in this precedent-shattering demonstration. Norris' sentiments were, perhaps, illustrative of the feelings of progressives throughout the country: "I left the chamber because it was the only way, in my helplessness, that I could show my condemnation of the disgraceful and unwarranted fight made to drive Senator Cutting out of public office. The determined opposition of the Democratic National Committee and its chairman to bring about the defeat of Senator

Cutting is the greatest case of ingratitude in history. It is a blot upon the record of the administration." When Huey Long later called for an investigation of the political activities of James Farley, some of the progressives in the Senate, Norris among them, sided with the Louisiana Senator, a man generally regarded by progressives as a fascist prototype.[19] Issuewise, progressives also deplored the leveling-off of the New Deal's relief and experimental measures. Men like Senator Norris, the La Follettes, and Governor Olson accused the government of refusing to support, if not actually opposing, the Connery thirty-hour work week bill, the St. Lawrence Seaway project, and veterans' cash bonus proposal. They charged the administration with becoming timid at a time when there was a clear need and mandate for bold action.

The President was alive to the possibilities inherent in the progressive complaints. Writing to Colonel Edward House in February, 1935, he enumerated three major camps of opponents to the Democratic party: the conservative Republicans, who might nominate Senator Vandenberg for President; the liberal Republicans, who might take a chance with the president of the University of Wisconsin, Glenn Frank; and the Progressives like La Follette, Cutting, and Nye, who he believed were toying with the idea of a third-party ticket. Roosevelt held that "all of these Republican elements are flirting with Huey Long and probably financing him. A third Progressive Republican ticket and a fourth

'Share the Wealth' ticket they believe would crush us and that then a free for all would result in which case anything might happen.

"There is no question that it is all a dangerous situation but when it comes to Show-down these fellows cannot all lie in the same bed and will fight among themselves with almost absolute certainty. They represent every shade."[20]

James Farley, in the meantime, was carrying on a campaign against the President's friendly relations with political mavericks and non-Democrats. The Democratic national chairman selected Floyd B. Olson as one of his prime targets. Farley sent annotated press clippings to the White House of almost every criticism of the administration made by the Minnesota governor. Typical was a story clipped from a Minnesota newspaper showing, to Farley's satisfaction, that Olson was disloyal to the President, an opportunist, and, to boot, unsound in his ideas.[21] The President remained publicly friendly, however, with the Wisconsin Progressives and the Minnesota Farmer-Laborites. These two groups continued to receive patronage and spoils from the national administration. This policy supposedly included the granting of $100,000,000 to Wisconsin to be used at Governor Philip La Follette's discretion to aid the people of the state.[22]

Many independent political groups were eager to exploit what appeared to be increasing popular dissatisfaction with the New Deal. In 1934 and 1935, the element in the Socialist party led by Norman

Thomas reinvigorated its efforts to initiate the establishment of a liberal-leftist front. Thomas believed that Socialists should try boldly to secure cooperation upon certain specific issues with the Communists and various political independents.[23] Conservative and even moderate Socialists—holding that the Communists were utterly untrustworthy—did not respond favorably to any proposal aimed at joint Socialist-Communist action. The Socialist national convention, meeting in Detroit in June, 1934, was racked with strife and dissension over the issue, no decision being reached.[24] When, in December, 1934, the national executive committee gave Socialists permission to arrange for limited joint action with Communists and Marxist "splinters" on state and local levels, the party suffered a rash of bitter factional fights.[25] Three months later, Norman Thomas expressed alarm at the attempts of Senator Huey Long and Father Charles Coughlin to capture the rising discontent. He urged Socialists to lead the drive for a Farmer-Labor-Unemployed party, because Long or Coughlin "will capture the movement if we don't." The Socialist national committee rejected Thomas' demand, deciding that prime attention had to be devoted to resolving the party's interfactional struggles.[26] The battles over Socialist-Communist relations were to absorb Socialist energies almost completely until the party's conservative wing seceded in 1936.[27]

By 1935, the Communist International organization sensed a world-wide drift toward increased liberal and radical political activity, which might be exploited for the benefit of the Kremlin. A new party line was, consequently, in the offing. The central theme of the Comintern meeting held in Moscow in August was that the battle against world fascism could be effective only with the formation of national united fronts of leftist and liberal elements. Georgi Dimitrov, the general secretary of the organization's executive committee, asserted that Communists would initially be subordinate in such movements in order to achieve working class unity. He contended that the Communists would naturally assume leadership as the task of disposing of fascism and capitalism became too great for united-front governments. Only by using the united-front technique, Dimitrov averred, "will the working class at the head of all the working people, welded into a million strong revolutionary army, led by the Communist International and possessed of so great and wise a pilot as our leader Comrade Stalin, be able to fulfill its historical mission with certainty." It was indicated by the Comintern leaders that a united-front party could be successful in the United States.[28] Earl Browder, the secretary of the American Communist party, immediately set about to conform to the new Comintern policy. Browder called for a party of workers and farmers in the United States, organized on the basis of a broader economic and political program than that recommended by the Communist party. This united-front organization was to be built around a platform which advocated social insurance, civil-

73

rights protection, increased public-works appropria-
tions, relief for farmers, government seizure and
operation of idle factories, severe modification of the
power of judicial review, abolition of inequitable
representation in the Senate, and relief of the poor
from taxation.[29] The publication of the Minnesota
Communist party, *United Action,* reflected the
change in the Communist party line. It declared that
the Communist party had taken the wrong attitude
toward the Minnesota Farmer-Laborites in the past;
that only the reactionaries and not the throngs of
sincere laborers and farmers had been seen among
the Farmer-Laborites. "As a result of this wrong understanding of the Farmer-Labor Party and the desires of its membership, the Communist Party iso-
lated itself from the Farmer-Labor Party masses instead of working with them in a common struggle for
the needs of the people."[30]

As for the leaders of the Minnesota Farmer-Laborites and the Wisconsin Progressives, their position was to retain their ties with the New Deal while
holding the door open for possible participation in
the Farmer-Labor Political Federation's new-national-party endeavors. As Philip La Follette put it:
"We are hoping that movements will develop in the
various states which can be put altogether into a co-
hesive whole. However, it seems doubtful if such a
condition can be forced ahead of its time."[31]
Throughout 1935, the Wisconsin governor reiter-
ated his opinion that liberals and radicals had to pro-
ceed most carefully in planning political realign-

ment. Senator Robert La Follette cautiously seconded him, expressing doubt as to the formation of a new party in 1936. Floyd Olson, who, like the La Follettes, was being subjected to intense pressure from the FLPF organizers, continued to "play footsy" with the new-party movement. Typical of Governor Olson's position was his assertion that "what's going to happen next year will determine whether there will be a national third party or not." Fiorello La Guardia also flirted with the new-party advocates. In 1934 and 1935, the New York mayor was often quoted as predicting a political realignment, although he was never specific as to how it was to be accomplished. La Guardia enjoyed close and friendly relationships with the Wisconsin Progressives, and, as a "multi-partisan" independent, frequently condemned the two major parties.[32]

The leaders of the Farmer-Labor Political Federation were convinced that conditions among the nation's progressives, radicals, and lower classes were such that they could be molded into a new national farmer-labor party. The road to this objective was, of course, fraught with obstacles. By instilling fresh life into the New Deal, the President could upset the Federation's plans. The Long and Coughlin groups, with their frantic and emotional appeals, could perhaps gain the affections of the discontented. Although it seemed unlikely, there was always the possibility that a La Follette or an Olson could start his own national party without consulting other independent progressives or radicals. Furthermore, the

Communists presented a very grave problem now that they had decided "to co-operate" in building a united-front movement. The principal goals of FLPF, therefore, were to launch the new party in time to allow for adequate planning of the strategy to be used in the 1936 campaign; to obtain commitments, as soon as possible, from mugwumps like the La Follettes and Olson, so that it would be difficult for them to return to Roosevelt's camp should the New Deal be liberalized; to organize the progressives and radicals in Congress in order to show that they could work together for a given and agreed-upon set of legislative objectives; and to continue to organize and to exploit economic, political, and social dissatisfaction wherever it might be found.

Looking forward to a legislative basis for political realignment, the FLPF estimated that some sixteen to twenty Democrats and eight to ten Republicans in the House might join the three Minnesota Farmer-Laborites and the seven Wisconsin Progressives. In the Senate, La Follette, Shipstead, and the six to eight other progressive-minded members might be swayed in favor of the new-party idea or at least toward increased legislative solidarity. In March, 1935, these progressive legislators gathered together to attempt agreement on legislative action. They theoretically agreed on certain points of legislative concentration: federal regulation of credit and currency, abolition of tax exemption for securities, increased gift and inheritance taxes, the Frazier-Lemke plan of farm refinancing, lower home loan interest rates, legislative guarantees of the cost of production and a reasonable profit for agriculture, effective restriction of laboring hours, guarantee of the right of collective bargaining, adequate public works, employment at a decent wage, federal aid for education, government ownership of natural resources and monopolies, elimination of war profits, "no foreign entanglements," illness and old-age insurance, unemployment compensation, full governmental protection of free speech and press, and regulations forbidding Congressional "gag" rules. It is fairly obvious that the major points of concentration agreed upon by the Congressional progressives resembled a full-fledged platform. Almost all of the special legislative interests of the participants in this progressive caucus were represented. The question was, would any one of these Congressmen devote as much time toward working for all the other points put together as he would for his own proposals? If the progressive Congressmen had lent enough support to one another's proposals and if they had all followed some strategic plan, they might well have met with substantial legislative success. But, because of continual argument concerning their formal party affiliations and their inability to subordinate their favorite individual interests to a basic group program, the efforts to achieve legislative solidarity largely failed. Perhaps the basis of their failure was the fact that the Congressional progressives far too often played the roles of prima donnas. They all seemed to be leaders and found it difficult to subordinate themselves for the common good. "It is precisely because of this," Thomas Amlie has stated, "that we did not have the progressive bloc we seemed to have."[33]

In view of the great variety of dissident groups which the Farmer-Labor Political Federation hoped to incorporate in the new party, its leaders attempted to be most cautious in planning their course of action. The idea that FLPF, as such, should call the first party convention was rejected. As Amlie wrote Howard Y. Williams: "Such a national meeting would have to be carefully engineered. It could not be sponsored by one group. It would be sure to result in failure. We do not want another national Epic movement. We do not want another La Follette party such as we had in 1924. We do not want a national trade union party or a national funny money or anything of that kind. And that is precisely what we are likely to have unless we use the greatest caution."[34]

In an endeavor to pave the way for representative Midwestern dissident participation in any future new-party organizing convention, Williams and Congressman Amlie arranged for a meeting of key Midwestern progressive-radical politicians.[35] This conference was held in St. Paul, early in December, 1934, under the auspices of FLPF. Some seventy delegates from Illinois, Iowa, Kansas, Minnesota, Montana, North Dakota, South Dakota, and Wisconsin attended. The task set before them was to discuss possible platform planks for the proposed new party. Sensing that the meeting, by being held in St. Paul, had the additional purpose of trying to force the hand of the Minnesota Farmer-Labor party, Emil Regnier, the party's campaign manager, asked Farmer-Laborite officials not to participate. The conference was snubbed by Regnier and Hjalmar Petersen, the newly elected Minnesota lieutenant-governor. Governor Floyd Olson, however, addressed the group. Olson urged more government aid to co-operative enterprises and lauded the FLPF objectives, stating that they aimed at not just a new deal, but also a "new deck." The conference came to the conclusion that the goals announced by FLPF in the past would probably serve as an excellent core for the platform of any new party which might be formed by progressives and radicals. The tenor of the meeting was that if Roosevelt went to the right, a new party of liberals and radicals would have to be formed; whereas, if he went to the left, it was doubted that the Democratic party would follow, so that FLPF would become an essential instrument in forming a new vehicle for the President.[36] The conference closed with the adoption of a resolution calling upon the Minnesota Farmer-Labor and the Wisconsin Progressive parties, along with Farmer-Labor federations in Iowa, Kansas, Michigan, Montana, North Dakota, and South Dakota, to sponsor a call for a national third-party convention. All other organizations interested in such a development were invited to participate.[37]

In May, 1935, another preliminary conference was secretly held, under FLPF auspices, to draw up specific plans for the national new-party conference. Presided over by Wisconsin Progressive Representative George Schneider, some seventy-five left-wing leaders from eleven states attended the meeting. It was agreed that Socialists, Progressives, Farmer-Laborites, unionists, agrarian leaders, Technocrats, and unattached liberals would be invited to attend a general conference, the purpose of which was to unite left-of-center independents for action leading to a new party in 1936. Communists and "fascists" were declared unwelcome.[38] The conference call was sent out early in June, 1935, and was signed by five Congressmen: Wisconsin Progressives Thomas Amlie and George Schneider, progressive Republicans Vito Marcantonio of New York and Byron Scott of California, and Minnesota Farmer-Laborite Ernest Lundeen. The conference, set to meet in Chicago on July 5 and 6, was to discuss the following principles:

1. That the old order is breaking down and must be replaced by an economic system which will substitute planning for chaos, service for profit, and abundance for poverty.

2. That the present national leadership of the old parties offers no hope to the people of the United States.

3. That united action of all the forces working for political and economic democracy is urgent in the present crisis.

4. That any action must be based upon a fundamental program striking at the roots of the profit system.[39]

The response to the call was favorable. Coming from more than thirty states, some three hundred representatives and observers were present from almost every progressive and radical organization in the country—including at least ten unions and four national farm organizations. Three Socialist party observers were also in attendance. In the keynote address, Representative Amlie declared that "we are organizing so that if a third party is inevitable in 1936 we will have the leadership ready. Our aim is to unite all the groups who want a change to come through the ballot box, which excludes the Communists." Alfred Bingham characterized the delegates as "a cross section of the native American radical movement," and as the "direct descendants of the Populist tradition . . . without the benefit of the European idea." Senator Gerald Nye also spoke to the delegates and was well received. The North Dakota legislator, who was seen as a possible third-party presidential candidate, thought that the organization forthcoming from this conference would "eventually become the second party." He warned the group, however, not to look for reform overnight: "Look ahead five, ten, or twenty years." Nye cautioned that a new party could not win in 1936, because liberal senators would fear that any support given it would split the liberal ranks, thus throwing the government back into the hands of the reactionaries.

The delegates decided to call for the establishment of a new party for the 1936 elections, a party which would be based on the principle of "production for use instead of for profit." The conference formed a new organization, the American Commonwealth Political Federation, to prepare for the coming of the new party. Thomas Amlie was elected chairman of the Federation; John H. Bosch, head of the Minnesota Farm Holiday Association, vice chairman; Alfred Bingham, editor of *Common Sense*, executive secretary; Paul H. Douglas, treasurer; and Howard Y. Williams, national organizer. The American Commonwealth Political Federation's executive committee included, among others, Congressmen Schneider and Lundeen, Judge John F. Wirds of Iowa, Frank Rosenblum, vice president of the Amalgamated Clothing Workers of America, and Henry Pratt Fairchild of New York University.

One interesting event at the meeting was that Representative Vito Marcantonio withdrew his support from the conference, and termed any third-party action at this time "premature." His withdrawal was perhaps connected with one of the two major controversies at the conference. These concerned the name of the organization which would emerge from the meeting, and the question of the participation of Communists in the organization. Midwesterners wanted the organizational name to include "farmer-labor," while the Eastern and Far Western representatives contended that the phrase meant absolutely nothing to them. Although the title American Commonwealth Political Federation was adopted, the Midwestern section of the organization continued to use the Farmer-Labor Political Federation label.[40] Ray McKaig and Thomas Amlie submitted a proposal to exclude Communists from the organization. The measure was tabled, with the interpretation that Communist party members could not join ACPF.

The ACPF platform was centered, as has been indicated, around the idea of "production for use." The slogan was not actually spelled out beyond saying that it meant full governmental encouragement for producers' and consumers' co-operatives, and "public ownership and operation of natural resources, transportation and communication, public utilities, mines, munition plants and basic industries." The more immediate demands of ACPF included the payment of union wages to those employed on public-works projects; elimination of the dole; and higher wages for all workers. The federal government was to provide for and to support maternity, infancy, education, illness, old-age, and unemployment insurance or aid plans. All workers were to be guaranteed the right to join the union of their own choice. Police and military units were to be forbidden from interfering in farm and labor strikes, while company unions and "yellow dog" contracts were to be outlawed. Farmers were to be assured their cost of production, and the preclusion of importing agricultural products that competed with domestic produce. Farm-debt refinancing at 1½ per cent interest was promised, along with liberal and uniform moratoria legislation for farms and homes. The ACPF platform also called for heavy taxes on large incomes, income from public bonds, gifts, inheritances, and corporate surpluses. The immediate cash payment of the veterans' bonus was recommended, along with "unified Federal ownership and operation of the banking system for the purpose of controlling the issue of currency and credit." Declaring its unqualified opposition to war, ACPF called for stronger international agencies to aid in effecting world co-operation for peace. A demand was voiced for federal aid to education, through a federal department of education, to equalize state educational facilities. Moreover, a constitutional amendment was proposed which would give Congress the sole power to determine and to provide for "the general welfare of the people." Lastly, the ACPF conference reaffirmed its faith in democratically controlled government, and demanded complete governmental protection of equal civil, economic, and political rights.[41]

The ACPF program reflected a realization that the United States had changed from a rural to an urban society, although it contained demands that had been voiced by every Midwestern protest group since the 1890's. Moreover, ACPF went one step further than its native radical predecessors. Its production-for-use theory called for a complete change in our economic system, not just for the formulation of specific remedies for immediate problems. ACPF's rationale was ably expressed by Thomas Amlie. "What we are now going through is more than a depression; . . . it represents a new phase of capitalism; and . . . the suffering and maladjustment we are now experiencing is to a large extent chronic." Amlie contended that most progressives agreed that capitalism neither could be saved nor was worth saving, yet they blithely sought ways to patch it up. He declared that the method of solving this contradiction was obvious. Logic required that progressives must give up all efforts to resuscitate capitalism, and instead work for the best possible replacement. This, he believed, would necessitate "a wholesale planning of the socially-owned machinery of production for the sole use and benefit of society."[42]

Commenting upon the Chicago conference, Upton Sinclair declared his opposition to third-party action in 1936. He based his stand on the grounds that it would be impossible to unite a voting majority behind a third-party presidential candidate, and that, by splitting the progressive vote, a new party might throw the election to Hoover, the hypothetical Republican candidate. "I freely admit the larger part of the Roosevelt program so far is a blunder, but I believe he has an open mind and an experimental temper."[43] The *New York Times* scored the ACPF platform as being too vague and not well thought out, and summed it up as "slogans are slogans."[44] Immediate Socialist reaction to the Chicago conference was divided. Norman Thomas felt that although ACPF was not a representative farmer-labor organization, its platform was promising. The *Socialist Call*, however, editorialized that the ACPF conference was "much ado about nothing." Several months later, the Socialist party executive committee declared that there was little hope for the effective unification of the forces of protest into a third party for the 1936 elections. Yet the committee did believe that popular sentiment for such a venture was increasing, and expressed great hope for a strong progressive-radical party in the future.[45] The *New Republic* approved most of the aims of the American Commonwealth Political Federation and complimented it for taking the initial action necessary to bringing big mass organizations together in a new party mold.[46] The *Nation* stated that the future of American politics was ultimately to revolve around the battle between "production for use" forces and finance capitalism. It said that development of third-party action was essential to the success of the "production-for-use" group. "We see the Chicago conference as an early milestone in this long development."[47] The conference program was greeted enthusiastically in some sections of the Far West. The *Boise Valley* (Idaho) *Herald* stated that the ACPF "platform clearly shows that the conference does not intend to prolong the agony of the decadent, wornout economic system."[48] Noting ACPF's unfavorable reaction to Communist participation in any new coalition party, William Z. Foster stressed that a party containing all farmers and workers, even Communists, was absolutely necessary in the fight against the world menace of fascism. The Communist party chieftain asserted that the Communists did not seek to control any American united-front endeavor; they only wanted to take their places "in the ranks."[49] *Christian Century*, exercising its usual caution, commented "so far, so good, and as a political weathervane the ACPF will un-

doubtedly serve a useful purpose. Whether or not
it will really lead a third party movement is another
question. It has yet to convince the public that it offers something very much better than the Roosevelt
policies."[50]

Chapter IV
TOWARD A FARMER-LABOR PARTY
IN 1936

The initial steps of the American Commonwealth Political Federation toward the formation of a new party were accompanied by the publication of a number of sympathetic economic and political books. John Dewey's *Liberalism and Social Action*,[1] based on a series of lectures, was seen by many as an attempt to give the new-party movement an instrumentalist philosophical foundation. Asserting that man had not properly applied his intellect to the exploitation and distribution of our resources, Professor Dewey felt that a democratically controlled regimentation of material and technological forces was essential to the release of man's creative energies. He urged liberals, as the one perceptive group in our society, to unite to utilize their brains, and, if need be, to use force, so that intelligent social reorganization could be accomplished. The alternatives he presented were either increasing social chaos or some form of fascism.[2]

Controlling Depressions, by Paul Douglas,[3] was presented as an expert analysis of modern capitalism. Professor Douglas was convinced that capitalism was unlikely to survive two or three more depressions. He averred that, because of its inefficiency and its inhumane and undemocratic tendencies, the country's big business economy would have to give way to some mixed-enterprise system. The University of Chicago professor maintained that small businessmen, wage-earners, farmers, and salaried people must disentangle themselves from their illogical alliance with monopolistic capitalism.[4] Only in this way, could there be any hope of salvaging the few virtues of free enterprise. Douglas recommended a large number of modifications in American capitalism which he felt would be of the greatest value to whatever economic system the country finally adopted.[5] Among these recommendations were increased public works, especially housing projects; governmental control of currency and credit; governmental facilitation of the movement of capital and labor from contracting to expanding industries; socialization of industrial enterprises which naturally tend to monopolistic price and production limitations; establishment of a comprehensive system of unemployment insurance; governmental financial aid to consumers, when necessary, to avoid underconsumption of material goods; and the establishment of co-operative workshops quite similar to those advocated by Robert Owen and Louis Blanc, where the unemployed might produce for their own needs. Douglas admitted that carrying out these ideas, especially the last one, might lead to the complete abolition of capitalism. He concluded, however, that this chance would have to be taken if the nation was democratically to achieve economic stability and to foster a higher general standard of living.[6]

Alfred M. Bingham and Selden Rodman were probably the most prolific writers among the ACPF intellectuals in giving support to the new-party idea in 1935 and 1936. Besides serving as the editors of *Common Sense,* Bingham and Rodman wrote extensively in other magazines of a progressive-radical cast. Their edition of *Challenge to the New Deal,*[7] a collection of provocative writings from *Common Sense,* served to introduce the analyses and ideas of the native radicals into many libraries and homes. The most influential and widely ·discussed political and economic inquiry produced by an ACPF intellectual was probably Bingham's *Insurgent America.*[8] This well-written volume drew heavily upon the ideas of Paul Douglas, Henry Pratt Fairchild, and John Dewey. Asserting the traditional progressive concern for the public interest, Bingham proceeded to urge the need for progressives and radicals to capture the "middle class" in America for the goal of social reconstruction:

"The fact that there is such wide currency to the idea of a 'public,' between and more important than 'capital' and 'labor,' is significant, for we are governed by ideas. We are what we think we are. And if the bulk of people, in a modern capitalistic country like the United States, think of themselves as being of the middle-class, having interests between those of 'capital' and 'labor,' then there is such a middle-class or middle group of classes.

"This 'public' has been sadly ignored by the radicals."[9]

It was quite clear to Bingham that Marxism, in all its guises, was quite repugnant to the American

middle class because it embraced the ideas of the inherent superiority of the lowest of the low and the inevitability of class struggle. He declared that middle-
class virtues were convertible in terms of the values
of the "social reconstructionists." He was convinced
that middle-class beliefs in egalitarian society, "do-
good" projects, and "boosterism" constituted a substantial basis for middle-class participation in radical-
progressive action. What, then, Bingham asked,
could be the foundation for an appeal to the middle
class? "It is security—security of income, security for
home and family, security for old age, security of position—that the middle-class type craves."[10] Bingham
warned that progressives and radicals must realize
that the middle class feels it has a stake in capitalism
only in so far as capitalism seems to offer security.
When capitalism has failed, as he declared it had,
then the middle class feels adrift. In America, only
the Co-operative Commonwealth or a form of fascism
could attract them. Obviously then, democratic and
effective social reconstruction could come about only
if the bulk of the American people—the middle
class—were won to the cause of the Co-operative
Commonwealth. The middle class, he felt, could be
convinced only by a confident, positive approach,
one which pledged devotion to security, abundance,
and those property rights possessed by the bulk of
citizens. Sentimentalism, piety, patriotism, and
"boosterism," therefore, should all play a part in the
progressive-radical appeal. Force was to be used only
to meet the violence used by those who refused to

91

respect the democratic process. Since the necessity for such force seemed very unlikely, "in the long run nothing is going to be so effective as old-fashioned political campaigning."[11] As for Bingham's concept of the political and economic goals of a new party, emphasis was placed on democratic action. Dictatorship he definitely ruled out as discouraging individual responsibility and initiative.[12] The economy was ultimately to be based on co-operative organizations, with a minimum of governmental control and co-ordination. Capitalism was to continue only in businesses dealing in oddities and custom-made goods. Thus, according to Bingham, could a society based on production for use rather than on production for profit be established in the United States.[13]

Yet literature could not win the country for the Commonwealth forces. Practical planning and careful handling of followers were essential. Overoptimism and undue pessimism had to be avoided. The officers of the American Commonwealth Political Federation undertook to make it clear that while a new party could not hope to win in 1936 it could secure a solid political footing. Thomas Amlie declared:

> In judging the present situation, we must not forget that we are living in a time when extremely rapid changes can take place. It is only a year ago that the elections of California and Washington demonstrated that it is possible to get the American people to think politically in terms of retaining or discarding the profit system. The formation of successful third parties in Minnesota and Wisconsin has demonstrated the political feasibility of a complete divorce

92

from the two old parties. In my opinion it should be possible for a third party in 1936 to secure a total vote of between five and ten million. If this were accomplished, the issue would then be clearly defined in every legislative district by 1938.

ACPF planned, according to Amlie, to continue encouraging the formation of state federations of those favoring the establishment of the co-operative commonwealth. It would also make strenuous efforts to develop more literature to recruit and to guide radicals.[14] Howard Y. Williams, the Federation's national organizer, added to Amlie's statements the prediction that a new production-for-use party would gain control of the national government by 1940. He noted heavy labor support for the idea of a new party and revealed that Columbus, Ohio, had already invited the Farmer-Labor convention to meet there in 1936.[15]

ACPF was given new encouragement by developments within the Democratic party. By late August, well-founded rumors about a conservative revolt within that party were circulating. William Randolph Hearst, Al Smith, Bainbridge Colby, and Governors Albert Ritchie of Maryland and Eugene Talmadge of Georgia were said to be planning to launch a "Jeffersonian Democratic party" to oppose Roosevelt. It was also stated that Hearst had proposed Smith's running against the President and the Republican candidate.[16] Perhaps as an attempt to placate the rebellious conservatives in his party, Roosevelt wrote a letter to Roy Howard, the head of the

Scripps-Howard newspaper chain, that boosted the hopes of the independent progressives and radicals. The President said that the basic program to combat the business depression "has now reached substantial completion, and the 'breathing spell' [for private enterprise] . . . is here—very decidedly so."[17] Representative Amlie promptly issued a statement declaring that "President Roosevelt's 'breathing spell' for American business . . . officially marks the end of New Deal liberalism." The Chief Executive's message to Mr. Howard reveals "that so far as the President is concerned the depression is practically over and the Administration intends to rest on its oars." Amlie charged that Roosevelt had closed his eyes to the problems of those millions of Americans who were unemployed or living on charity. It was held that this new policy constituted a major blunder, because the President's political popularity was mainly founded on the promise that he would accomplish something basic for the people.[18]

ACPF met with a measure of organizational success in the various states in 1935. In the spring of that year, at the urging of Bingham and Amlie, Fusionist, Socialist, Knickerbocker Democrat, Technocrat, and labor elements had joined together to form the Commonwealth Federation of New York. This group was encouraged to do yeoman service in behalf of ACPF. Howard Y. Williams and Thomas Amlie were active throughout the nine months following the Chicago conference in aiding the organization of other commonwealth federations in the various sections of the country. By the summer of 1936, ACPF had organized or infiltrated third parties in California, Iowa, Kansas, Michigan, New Hampshire, and South Dakota, and had ties with commonwealth or farmer-labor associations in thirteen other states. Six other states had farm, labor, or Socialist groups working for the political and economic objectives of ACPF. In most of the remaining states of the union, the American Commonwealth Political Federation had local organizers. Many of these groups were weak in membership but they offered a pattern of organization that would be necessary for the new-party advocates to make a formal appeal to the electorate.[19]

One of the more interesting organizational activities of ACPF was the consolidation of the progressive and radical forces in Wisconsin. It was apparent, following the formation of the Wisconsin Progressive party, that the left-of-center farm and labor groups were dissatisfied with the "La Follette control" of the party. ACPF aided the non-La Follette progressives and radicals of the state to unite, with the hope that they would soon assume control of the Progressive party. This non-La Follette coalition, called the Farmer-Labor Progressive Federation, was established in December, 1935, on the basis of the production-for-use program. The Federation was sponsored by the Wisconsin State Federation of Labor, the Farmer-Labor Partisan League, the Wisconsin Railway Brotherhoods, the Farmers' Equity Union, the Wisconsin Cooperative Milk Pool, the

Wisconsin Farm Holiday Association, the Wisconsin Workers' Alliance, the state Socialist party, and representatives of the Wisconsin Progressive party. The Farmer-Labor Progressive Federation made it possible for these organizations to pledge their political support to the Progressive party in exchange for the right to participate in determining the party's policy and candidates. In this federation, the state's left-wingers could maintain the autonomy of their various organizations and yet speak as a unit in political matters. The members of these organizations, with the exception of the Socialist party, which joined as a group, were to join the Federation as individuals. Dues of one dollar a person were charged, and discipline was maintained by threat of expulsion. Illustrative of the attitude of the member groups was the editorial comment of *Kenosha Labor:* "Together they will make the most powerful political family in the state, and one that will likely have a decisive voice in the affairs of the nation within five years."[20] The Minnesota Farmer-Labor party presented no such problem of organization. The state's radical unions and agrarians were already merged politically in the form of the Farmer-Labor Association, which effectively participated in the formulation of party policies.

Although ACPF worked energetically with both the Wisconsin and Minnesota movements, it had to choose which of the two should issue the call for a 1936 national third-party convention. ACPF officials finally decided to work through the Minnesota

Farmer-Laborites largely because their leader, Floyd Olson, was not only warming up to the new-national-party idea but was becoming increasingly attractive to all wings of the progressive-radical movement. The Minnesota governor was an American radical in that he was probably the chief exponent of a co-operative economic system. Olson had declared that rugged individualism was dead, contending that "in a new social order that is vital to the future economic security of our nation, it is imperative that consumers organize cooperatively along with similar organizations of producers." He pointed out that if trusts and interlocking directorates are advantageous to private greed, they should also, if used co-operatively, "insure economic justice to the masses."[21] Minnesota, under Olson's leadership, provided more aid and encouragement to co-operatively owned and managed enterprises than any other American state. From his inauguration as governor in 1931 to mid-1935, 663 co-operatives, operating in thirty-eight fields from seeds to burial, beer to theatricals, and insurance to dairy produce, had been established. Minnesota, through its state institutions of higher education and the state department of agriculture, had sponsored a comprehensive educational program dealing with the problems of co-operatives.[22] Minnesota also protected its natural resources in an energetic fashion under Olson, and the governor demanded, without success, state operation and ownership of public utilities. Failing there, his administration smoothed the way for increased state regulation

97

and municipal ownership of public utilities. In the latter respect, Minnesota ranked first among the states in the percentage of publicly generated electric power.[23] Olson was not disdainful of socialization or nationalization on the federal level, but he was definitely opposed to national concentration of economic power, be it under private or governmental auspices. In this, the Minnesotan voiced the views of most advocates of the Co-operative Commonwealth.

Politically, as has been noted, Governor Olson was growing more friendly toward ACPF and its goals. In a speech to 1,500 persons at the November, 1935, meeting of the New York Commonwealth Federation, he flatly declared that the ideal of profits second and needs first could not be achieved with either of the two traditional parties. The governor stated that "the Democratic party, despite its desire for reform, is trying to make a system click that cannot click. You can't have abundance with a capitalistic system. You can't have profits and have abundance. There must be a third party in the United States." Olson urged that all labor and farm organizations, including the AFL, must soon become units in a new party, so that "when the time comes, in 1936 or 1940, we will have a fighting force in the United States to elect members of Congress and possibly a President of the United States." Although the Minnesotan demurred at the idea of his candidacy for President in 1936 because of his commitment to run for the Senate, he contended that the possibilities were good for the formation of a national farmer-labor ticket in that year.[24] The next day, in a pungent address over the Columbia Broadcasting System, Olson advised the youth of the nation to join ACPF so that they might gain a new and just economic system. He asserted that the young people of the United States cannot help but fail under the present system because "the game is fixed; the dice are loaded."[25]

After several months of pressure and publicity in Minnesota, the American Commonwealth Political Federation officially moved to have the Minnesota Farmer-Labor party issue the call for a third-party convention in 1936. Alfred Bingham, ACPF executive secretary, asked Governor Olson to move the official affiliation of their two organizations—as Olson had promised in December, 1935—and also to encourage his party to promote the possibility of a new-national-party movement. There was, evidently, little doubt on the part of ACPF that the Minnesota Farmer-Labor party and its titular head would join in the formation of a new party in 1936. The rub was whether the Farmer-Laborites would support the entering of a presidential ticket. Bingham wrote that when Olson and he had last conferred in November, 1935, the governor was still undecided whether there should be a presidential ticket in 1936. He informed Olson that the national executive committee of ACPF wanted every effort to be made to nominate a new-party candidate for President. Bingham declared that the committee realized the danger that the launching of a presidential campaign in 1936 might fail miserably and result in wholesale disillusionment of the third-party forces. He felt, however, that this danger could be avoided "provided we do nothing from which we cannot later withdraw. The danger of not taking advantage of latent possibilities this year is that the national third party movement, having no dramatic center or head, will remain impotent for several years more, during which time the forces of fascism and reaction will be organizing. The future of this country may very well depend upon the extent to which the new party becomes a reality this year. The risk of inaction is too great to be ignored."[26] The success and substance of a new party, the ACPF executive secretary contended, rested in large part upon the action of the Minnesota Farmer-Laborites in their March, 1936, convention. He believed that if the Farmer-Labor party called not only for a new national party but also for a presidential slate, the Wisconsin Progressives would support the movement. With both Minnesota and Wisconsin "pushing," Bingham asserted that third-party sentiment in the Middle and Far West would boil over. He also felt that because of the great possibility the Supreme Court would declare the Wagner and Guffey labor statutes unconstitutional, "the labor movement may make a complete shift."[27]

On another front, the *New Republic* accelerated its support of the new-party movement throughout the winter and spring of 1936. By April, because of what it saw as the increasing danger of fascism and economic reaction, the magazine urged the prompt establishment of a new party with or without a presidential candidate.[28] The *Nation* was more cautious, calling only for the formation of a political organization or party which would work for the election of a large bloc of progressive-radical Congressmen. Such a group of legislators would be able to work cohesively for social advancement and to keep the administration from veering toward reaction or dictatorship. It would be out of the question for any farmer-labor group to put up a nominee for President in 1936. The *Nation* looked forward to a full and effective farmer-labor ticket in 1940 or 1944.[29]

Common Sense, the semi-official organ of ACPF, in surveying the political scene for 1936, deprecated Socialist and labor reluctance to join wholeheartedly in moving for the new party. It noted that although the Socialist party had tentatively decided to run its own 1936 ticket, the party rank-and-file had voted five-to-one in support of the farmer-labor party idea. It also observed that the persecuted members of the Southern Tenant Farmers' Union had demanded the establishment of a state farmer-labor party in at least Arkansas. As for organized labor, *Common Sense* observed that it seemed still to adhere to Roosevelt, but added that "a lot of desperate voters, without vested interests, are demanding someone to vote for in 1936."[30] It admitted that the great majority of dissidents might choose to stand by an established political force like the New Deal rather than switch over to an unknown quantity. If this happened, a

101

farmer-labor presidential candidate might poll less than three million votes. This could ruin the movement's chances in the future, for "in a land that worships success, a new party must show it can succeed." Yet, the magazine asserted, this possibility should not deter the new-party advocates from action in 1936.

It may be far more dangerous to overlook the dynamic elements in the present situation, and do nothing. The most one can do without a presidential candidate is not very far from nothing. It is only in a national campaign, when all eyes are focused on the great national issues, that the many local and state movements can be swept into a dramatic national crusade.

Then again, to wait, means to leave the field open to all comers. It means that these precious political potentialities, as and if they materialize, will be captured by others with inadequate or misleading programs. Fascists like Talmadge are fishing in the troubled waters, and might become the champions of the desperate if there were no other champions. . . . And finally, the greatest danger in inactivity, may lie in the swift economic disintegration that may come in the years between 1936 and 1940, with no strong party in the field able to leap to the rescue. Every indication points to growing unemployment, growing debts, with the possibility of a deep decline when confidence in recovery is shattered beyond hope. And the grim threat of war is never far distant. *There may well be no election of 1940*.[31]

Further to reassure the weak and to stimulate the flagging, *Common Sense* gave its survey of the variable estimate of what a farmer-labor presidential candidate might receive in the way of ballots, "not considering the possibility of a landslide":

102

	Minimum	*Maximum*
Minnesota	300,000	500,000
Wisconsin	300,000	500,000
California	250,000	800,000
Oregon	100,000	200,000
Washington	150,000	300,000
labor vote	500,000	2,000,000
farm vote	500,000	2,000,000
Townsendites	500,000	1,000,000
Socialists, etc.	300,000	1,000,000
anti-war, etc.	500,000	2,000,000
	3,400,000	10,300,000

Common Sense asserted that this estimated vote would give a farmer-labor party the electoral votes of from at least two to four states, a good base upon which to build for victory in 1940.[32]

In the winter and spring of 1936, ACPF was affected by activities on the peripheries of dissent. The Townsend movement, which previously had avoided entanglement with political parties, severely criticized the two old parties for neglecting Dr. Francis Townsend's old-age relief program and for investigating his organization in Congress. Late in 1935, the Townsend group's convention passed a resolution calling for third-party action. Townsend himself publicly discussed the idea of third-party action in 1936 to gain fair consideration of his plan. Active interest in capturing the old-age segment of the electorate, and especially the Townsend movement, was shown by ACPF.[33] The Communist drive for a farmer-labor party was moved into high gear in 1936. Earl Browder, speaking over the Columbia

Broadcasting System, asked all Americans to join in a party of agrarians and workers to smash the rule of Wall Street. Speaking for his party, he vowed that "we propose no actions except those which the American people are prepared to organize and carry out themselves in their own interests." Alfred Bingham, on behalf of ACPF, immediately issued a statement condemning Browder's plea, asserting that it would confuse public thinking. Bingham pointed out that until 1935 the Communist party had vigorously opposed the establishment of a farmer-labor party.[34]

Meanwhile, forces were at work that would bring the Farmer-Labor Convention of 1936 into being. Howard Y. Williams announced that he would formally request the Minnesota Farmer-Laborites, in their biennial convention in March, to issue a call for the new national party. Both he and Bingham stated their conviction that a new party would launch a full national ticket. Williams proposed that Senator Nye be the party's candidate for President.[35] At the Minnesota Farmer-Labor convention, Governor Olson asserted that he was willing to join with other groups in forming a new party in the United States. He felt that the party could run candidates for Congress, but he told the delegates that the question of nominating a candidate for President was for them to decide. A formal resolution was adopted 368½ to 215½ by the Minnesota convention, reaffirming the "necessity of building State Farmer-Labor parties and a national Farmer-Labor party." The resolve directed that "a special committee be elected with representation from each Congressional district to call a conference of and to cooperate with other progressive labor, farmer and political organizations and leaders in calling a national conference to explore the possibilities of a national Farmer-Labor ticket in 1936 and in promoting State Farmer-Labor parties, a concerted campaign to elect Farmer-Labor Congressmen in the 1936 campaign, and in building a national Farmer-Labor party."[36] By mid-April of 1936, the special committee had formulated plans to aid third-party men in other states. A delegation of six Farmer-Laborites, including Paul A. Harris, the Farmer-Labor state chairman, was appointed to represent the party at the forthcoming new-party convention. The committee felt that if an active 1936 campaign was waged by a national farmer-labor party, thirty-five to forty of its candidates could be elected to Congress. The formal national convention call was issued by the Minnesota Farmer-Labor party early in May. The call invited all liberals to gather at the Morrison Hotel in Chicago, May 30-31, to accomplish the following aims: (1) to devise methods of aiding local and state farmer-labor parties; (2) to unify farmer-labor and progressive groups for the building of a national liberal party; (3) to discuss the advisability of running a presidential candidate in 1936; and (4) to prepare to run an active campaign, at least on state levels.[37]

After years of work, everything finally appeared to be arranged for the formation of the new party. At the eleventh hour, however, irresolvable situations

105

arose to confront the forthcoming Chicago convention. One of these concerned Communist participation in the new party. While Communists had not been allowed to join ACPF, their united-front appeal seemed to be winning converts among the Federation's affiliates. This led to many bitter arguments behind the scenes. Moreover, while the Socialist party had shown signs of increased interest in farmer-labor action early in 1936, party members generally decided to ignore the Chicago convention. Their position was usually explained on the ground of not wishing to be associated politically with Communists or of concluding that a national farmer-labor party could not be successful in 1936. Dr. Townsend, by May, had also decided not to co-operate with ACPF in political action. Moreover, the leader of the Farm Holiday Association, the fiery Milo Reno, died early in May. His death severed one of the strongest links between the third-party movement and the radical agrarian element.[38]

The most important issue, however, facing the Chicago convention concerned the nomination of a presidential candidate. In this, the Chicago convention and the potential third-party men were most strongly influenced by the activities of Labor's Non-Partisan League and the American Liberty League. The American Liberty League had been established by conservatives in 1934 as "the spokesman for a business civilization." Politically, the Liberty League's goal was to insure that complete financial and propaganda support would be available to a

106

conservative presidential candidate in 1936 in the contest with Roosevelt and any other "leftist" nominees.[39] Progressives, liberals, and radicals were repeatedly warned, by the President's lieutenants and especially by the newly-formed Labor's Non-Partisan League, as to the "reactionary" consequences which might result from the Liberty League's endeavors. It is interesting to note that two of the goals of Labor's Non-Partisan League were to prevent the naming of a third-party, Farmer-Labor presidential candidate, and to encourage discord in the Socialist party.[40] The Communist "menace" was also emphasized by some of the Chief Executive's supporters, with the able assistance of the rather clumsy intrigues of the Communist party itself. Adding these things together, the nation's progressives and radicals reassessed the character and accomplishments of Roosevelt. The great majority of them decided that they had no alternative other than sticking with the President. This was well illustrated late in May, when Floyd Olson suddenly instructed Farmer-Laborites to boycott the Chicago convention if it voted to nominate a national ticket in 1936. The Minnesota governor also dispatched a message to be read to the delegates warning that a farmer-labor presidential nominee might cause Roosevelt's defeat and consequently elect a "fascist Republican."[41] As far as the Minnesota Farmer-Labor party and ACPF were concerned, the endorsement of Roosevelt by Labor's Non-Partisan League definitely forced the Chicago Convention to concentrate on strategy leading to running tickets for the House and the Senate. On the eve of the convention even Howard Y. Williams had to admit that barring something unusual there would be no consideration of a presidential nominee at the Chicago meeting. Williams repeated, of course, the shibboleth that a new-party presidential ticket would be ready for the next presidential campaign.[42]

The Chicago convention had been scheduled to hear such nationally known speakers as John L. Lewis, Thomas Amlie, Louis Waldman, Alfred Bingham, and Paul Douglas. Owing to the collapse of the factors which would lend political significance to the meeting, however, all hope of getting leaders of labor to attend was crushed. Men like David Dubinsky decided at the last moment to skip the conference, although they sent representatives to carry their messages of "sympathy" and "interest." Louis Waldman, one of the key right-wing Socialist leaders, also decided to stay at home, in order to battle further moves by his party's radicals to grab complete control of the Socialist organization. The last-minute refusals of Amlie, Bingham, and Douglas to participate in the convention practically killed the meeting before it started. Apparently speaking for the three ACPF leaders, Amlie condemned the conference as being seemingly "under the domination of Communists." Williams, who was less opposed to the united-front idea and who felt that the Communists could be kept under control, stuck with the experiment. The paucity of effective leadership present at Chicago also rendered ineffective most of the efforts that were made outside of Wisconsin and Minnesota to elect Farmer-Labor Congressmen in 1936.[43]

The convention, divested of its political potential, met as scheduled. Scattered union and farmer representatives joined with Williams and most of the regular ACPF delegates to carry on. Representatives of the Minnesota Farmer-Labor party and Labor's Non-Partisan League were on hand to see that the President would not be hurt politically by the meeting. Some other leaders of national stature, like John Bosch, the new chief of the sadly depleted National Farm Holiday Association, also attended. Earl Browder and Clarence Hathaway, editor of the *Daily Worker,* were present, pumping for the united-front doctrine.[44] About the only piece of good news that the third-party men were to hear during the course of the Chicago meeting was that EPIC had voted to co-operate with the Farmer-Labor movement if it established a new party.[45] This shot-in-the-arm, however, was far from enough to renew the spirits of the assembled progressive and radical representatives. Williams substituted for Amlie as the convention's keynote speaker, attempting to strike a theme that could appeal to all elements of the movement—namely, that of the war menace which was threatening the world. In a statement that was sure to be approved by many progressives and radicals, he called for the use of the universal strike to stop war. Roger Rutchick, the Deputy Attorney General of Wisconsin, was elected permanent chairman of the convention. The eighty-four delegates, representing twenty-eight states, listened—and adhered—to the reading of Floyd Olson's plea that the meeting should not run a candidate in opposition to Roosevelt. Then two main questions were put to the delegates: (1) Should Communists be allowed to participate in the convention and in any organization which might issue from its deliberations? (2) Should a formal convention call to launch a farmer-labor party that year be approved by the meeting? On the former proposal, the action of the meeting was to table it, which thus allowed Communists free rein in the meeting. The latter resolve was referred to committee, where, led by J. B. C. Hardman, the Amalgamated Clothing Workers' representative, a fierce battle took place to kill it. It was forced out of committee at the insistence of veteran progressive Judge Edward Jeffries of Detroit, Mrs. Victor Berger, and John Bosch. Jeffries persuaded the committee to recommend the calling of a farmer-labor party organizing convention, to be held in Detroit not later than September 5, convincing the committee members that the Minnesota and Wisconsin third parties could not live much longer without a national affiliation. When this recommendation was brought before the convention, it was for all practical purposes killed by amending it so as to leave the convention call to the discretion of the Minnesota Farmer-Labor party and an "advisory council" of farm, labor, and other organizations participating in the Chicago convention. Having bet on the New Deal horse for

110

the year 1936, the Minnesota organization failed to call for the organizing convention, thus blocking any action that might have been taken by the "advisory council."[46]

Writing its own epitaph, the moribund farmer-labor meeting issued the following program of principles intended to guide future political action by the nation's progressives and radicals: (1) the abolition of monopoly; (2) public ownership of natural resources; (3) an effective and adequate federal social security plan financed by increased taxes on large incomes, inheritances, gifts, and corporate surpluses; (4) a thirty-hour work week with no pay reduction; (5) the use of a union wage scale on public-works projects; (6) long-term farm mortgages; (7) government financing of farm debts at 1½ per cent interest; (8) opposition to crop reduction; (9) the enactment of legislation to curb the powers of the Supreme Court and to "reassert the power of Congress to enact adequate social and labor legislation"; and (10) effective opposition to war but support for the principles of collective security.

The platform was silent on banking, tariff, currency, child labor, and public housing, and had rejected the production-for-use idea. As a sign of the period, the convention went on record as demanding the governmental ownership and operation of factories manufacturing the implements of war, and as favoring the conscription of wealth in the event of war. The farmer-labor delegates also called for the unrestricted right of organization of trade unions,

111

and of striking and picketing; they stated their opposition to company unions and the use of coercive
measures against labor. The convention advocated
"a measure that will provide adequate funds for a
youth program that can give youth the opportunity
for education and work." Opposing any restriction of
those civil liberties guaranteed by the Constitution,
the delegates condemned any form of persecution,
formal or informal, of Negroes and the foreign-
born.[47] The platform, which attracted little attention because of the lack of significant organizational
support for it, represented in the main an ideological
step backward. Norman Thomas described it as one
of the worst "reformist" platforms ever offered, one
based "on the false philosophy of government under
capitalism as a Santa Claus with a subsidy for all."
The Socialist leader also implied that the platform
represented the results of Communist manipulation
at Chicago.[48] Even though the Chicago convention
was politically impotent before it was held, the Communist party still clung to it as an instrument with
which the united front might be achieved. The
Daily Worker, in demanding the immediate launching of the Farmer-Labor Party, exhorted: "Let us
unite behind the proposals of the national Farmer-
Labor conference." Later, the Communist Central
Committee indicated its support of the convention
and its platform.[49]

For all practical purposes, the resounding failure
of the farmer-labor party conference in 1936 signaled
the disintegration of the third-party movement

which had been sponsored by the League for Independent Political Action and its two successor organizations, the Farmer-Labor Political Federation and the American Commonwealth Political Federation. John Dewey and Oswald Garrison Villard, along with most of the original sponsors of the movement, had, by 1936, either retired to the sidelines or gone on to new causes. Disillusioned with the "prima donnas" of the progressive-radical element, Thomas Amlie was to swing over to Roosevelt's camp, making it clear that he was supporting the President as the least of many evils. Howard Y. Williams was to continue, for a while longer, to campaign for the idea of a national farmer-labor party. Alfred Bingham, in the editorial columns of *Common Sense,* reluctantly accepted Roosevelt as the only possible choice in 1936. By 1939, Bingham and Williams, along with Paul Douglas, became supporters of the President.[50]

Thus this third-party movement died. For almost seven years, it had been striving to achieve the consolidation of the nation's progressive-radical elements in a new political party. The attempts of LIPA to accomplish this end for action in the 1932 elections had been frustrated by its own inability to sell its theories, and by the rise to prominence of Roosevelt. LIPA and its offspring, FLPF and ACPF, renewed these efforts between 1932 and 1936, not without heartening results. The slackening pace of the New Deal and the increasing successes of the new-party advocates, gave hope that the solidarity of progressives and radicals would be realized by 1936. The

113

hard labor which had been invested in fostering state and local affiliates, converting members of the established organs of protest and discontent and educating dissidents in general, seemed to be yielding dividends. And yet, ironically enough, a few months after the movement began to be recognized as politically prominent, it plunged irretrievably into insignificance. Although other endeavors were to be made to form a new liberal-radical party in the 1930's, one could not help questioning that they would succeed where this promising movement failed.

Chapter V
GOD'S ANGRY MEN

During Roosevelt's first term as President, the nation saw the rise to prominence of many men who had hitherto been politically obscure. One group of this political *nouveau riche*, Father Charles E. Coughlin, Representative William Lemke, the Rev. Gerald L. K. Smith, and Dr. Francis Townsend, attempted to capitalize upon their fame by forming or supporting a new "radical" party in 1936—the Union party. Good arguments may be submitted for excluding consideration of this organization in a study which deals largely with radicals and progressives, since the party has been frequently labeled "fascist." Yet there were similarities between the Union party and the other movements treated in this study, aside from their involvement in independent political action. These similarities mainly centered on the fact that all the movements appealed to similar groups— the lower economic classes and those who felt themselves to be progressives or radicals.

Selden Rodman has pointed out that the progenitors of the Union party were trying to capture the "masses" on the basis of a program which, in large part, had been borrowed from native progressives and radicals.[1] Time and time again after the 1934 elections, officials of the Farmer-Labor Political Federation, the American Commonwealth Political Federation, and the Socialist party warned against their maneuvers in this direction. It is interesting to note that the Union party was to nominate for President a veteran battler for farmer-labor causes, a man who had been one of the guiding forces behind the old Nonpartisan League, Congressman William Lemke. Milo Reno, the leader of the radical Farm Holiday Association and one who co-operated with the other third-party movements, showed that he was attracted by men like Coughlin and Townsend. In the spring of 1935, Reno stated that he hoped they would unite with Senator Huey Long to end "wage slavery."[2] After the announcement of Lemke's candidacy, the president of the National Farmers' Union, an organization which was usually in strong sympathy with progressive aims, predicted that the 250,-000 members of his group "very largely will support . . . Lemke."[3] Father Coughlin's warm advocacy of the cause of the Automotive Industrial Workers' Association before 1936, had won him many friends in the ranks of labor.[4] Moreover, many of the Wisconsin Progressives and the Minnesota Farmer-Laborites expressed their sympathy or admiration for the men who were to launch the Union party. For example, a staunch Farmer-Laborite like Henry Teigan was to write that, although he disagreed with Coughlin's views regarding the Italo-Ethiopian conflict and the Mexican government, he felt the goals of the National Union for Social Justice, more than those of any other organization in the country, resembled the program of the Minnesota Farmer-Labor party. Teigan further declared that the Detroit priest had been magnificent in his attempts to create popular sentiment for public ownership of banking institutions and public utilities.[5] The amount of sympathy within the Minnesota and Wisconsin third parties in 1936 was perhaps indicated in that while they declined to join forces with the Union party, they officially expressed their respect for the liberal elements at work within the Unionist ranks.[6] Furthermore, it should be observed that one out of every six-and-one-half votes cast for Representative Lemke in 1936 came from these two states.[7]

The main distinguishing feature of the Union party is to be discovered in the unusual personalities of the men who created it—namely, Senator Huey Long (who was to be the party's martyr and "patron saint"), Father Coughlin, Dr. Townsend, the Rev. Mr. Smith, and Congressman Lemke. The difference between these persons and men like Amlie, Bingham, Williams, Dewey, Olson, and the La Follette brothers was fundamental. The former group seemed to base their economic, political, and social arguments mainly on emotionalism, while the latter usually stressed the appeal to reason. An Amlie endeavored to persuade the forces of discontent toward the goals which he favored, while a Long attempted to use fire and brimstone to bring the malcontented to political "salvation." Since personalities were so important in the establishment and the campaign of the Union party, special attention will be given to its leaders: Coughlin, Long, Smith, Townsend, and Lemke.

Charles E. Coughlin, who had been educated at some of the best American and European universities, at the outset of the depression entered the ranks of the nation's vocal economic dissidents. Within a few years, the priest had gained a reputation around Detroit as a powerful advocate of an economic system which would reward man for work rather than for cunning and scheming. Coughlin hopped on the Roosevelt bandwagon in the 1932 campaign, and by 1933 was regarded as a leading defender of the President's economic program. Throughout 1933 and most of 1934, he corresponded frequently with the Chief Executive, giving advice and encouragement. The President was continually referred to as "the Boss" in Coughlin's letters; these messages were replete with laudatory phrases such as "he [Roosevelt] is magnificent."[8] In public, Coughlin was an ardent defender of the President. When the American Federation of Labor questioned the progress that had been made by the recovery program Coughlin characterized its criticism as being part of the "Stop Roosevelt" movement. He attacked the labor organizations as being controlled by gangsters, and declared, "Stop Roosevelt[?] stop him from being stopped."[9] Throwing the mantle of divine right around Roosevelt's shoulders, Coughlin, in testimony before the House Coinage, Weights, and Measures Committee, asserted that "President Roosevelt is not going to make a mistake, for God Almighty is guiding him." The priest went on to prophesy that a revolution would take place if Roosevelt's recommendations for remonetization of silver were not enacted. "It is either Roosevelt or ruin."[10]

A few days later he was quoted as saying that "it is high time the people of this nation begin to believe in what Mr. Roosevelt says. He is not a poet; he is most practical."[11] And so Coughlin's statements ran throughout most of 1933 and 1934. They were to change dramatically, though, and by 1936, the new line that he was to take was to be as extreme in opposition to Roosevelt as the old one had been in praising the President.

In November, 1934, the priest took the first step toward a complete break with the President. At that time, Coughlin founded the National Union for Social Justice, which was described as "a group of citizens not only dissatisfied with the sham politics and sham policies existing in America, but anxious for a cleansing of both political parties."[12] It should be emphasized that instead of offering encouragement and guidance to a spontaneous organization of the discontented by the discontented, Coughlin offered them a ready-made organization and ideology. Throughout the existence of the National Union, any form of real participation by the membership in its decision-making processes seemed to be lacking. The promulgated statement of principles and beliefs, to which members of NUSJ were to subscribe, was as follows:

1. The right of liberty of conscience and liberty of education, not permitting the state to dictate either my worship to my God or my chosen avocation in life.

2. Every citizen willing to work and capable of working shall receive a just and living annual wage which will

enable him to maintain and educate his family according to the standards of American decency.

3. Nationalising those public necessities which by their very nature are too important to be held in the control of private individuals—by these are meant, banking, credit and currency, power, light, oil, natural gas and all other natural resources.

4. Private ownership of all other property.

5. Upholding the right to private property yet of controlling it for the public good.

6. The abolition of the privately owned Federal Reserve Banking system and [the establishment of] a government owned Central Bank.

7. Rescuing from the hands of private owners the right to coin and regulate the value of money which right must be restored to Congress where it belongs.

8. One of the chief duties of this government owned Central Bank is to maintain the cost of living on an even keel and the repayment of dollar debts with equal value dollars.

9. The cost of production plus a fair profit for the farmer.

10. Not only the right of the laboring man to organize in unions but also in the duty of the Government which that laboring man supports, to protect these organizations against the vested interests of wealth and intellect.

11. The recall of all non-productive bonds and thereby in the alleviation of taxation.

12. The abolition of tax-exempt bonds.

13. The broadening of the base of taxation founded upon the ownership of wealth and the capacity to pay.

14. The simplification of government, and the further lifting of crushing taxation from the slender revenues of the laboring class.

15. In the event of a war for the defense of our nation

120

and its liberties, if there shall be a conscription of men, there shall be a conscription of wealth.

16. Preferring the sanctity of human rights to the sanctity of property right. . . . The chief concern of government shall be for the poor, because, as it is witnessed, the rich have ample means of their own to care for themselves.[13]

In the meantime, Senator Huey Long was attracting national attention. Long was a professional politician, whose career in public life started in 1918, when he was twenty-five years old. His economic and social philosophy, it seems, was used primarily to win political power. Its first significant use was in 1924, when Long ran practically a one-man door-to-door campaign in the Democratic gubernatorial primary against candidates of the well-organized state and New Orleans machines. Using his gifts of oratorical prowess and salesmanship to appeal to the poor whites of Louisiana, he attacked the wealthy industrialists and businessmen as enemies of the poor; he called for free school books and the construction of concrete highways throughout the state; he demanded a reduction in taxes on the lower economic classes; and he promised to let the poor folk of the rural areas hunt and fish without charge. Long lost this election, but he led both of his opponents in the rural areas of Louisiana despite heavy rains which rendered many country roads impassable. Perfecting his appeal to the state's citizens and gaining new political supporters as a result of his showing in the 1924 campaign, Long was able to win the governor's seat in 1928. Using every means at his disposal—including the fulfillment of many election promises, which was antithetical to the Louisiana political tradition—he was able to neutralize the remnants of the old machines and to build his own extremely well-oiled machine. Elected to the United States Senate in 1930, within a few years Long established a virtual dictatorship in the state. In national politics, the Senator from Louisiana energetically worked for Roosevelt in the 1932 Democratic convention. Long pledged his continued support of Roosevelt after his nomination, but the Louisianian warned that he stood ready to "expose" any attempts by the presidential candidate to "step out of line" to become a corporation tool.[14]

Long began to strive in earnest for national political prominence in 1933, motivated by personal ambition and a desire to focus Louisiana's attention on issues other than the questionable aspects of his state regime. The Senator offered a plan for national recovery and permanent prosperity which was called the "Share-Our-Wealth" program. It was given wide publicity in pamphlets and formed the theoretical basis for the establishment of Share-Our-Wealth clubs throughout the nation. The tenets of the plan were:

1. All personal fortunes over $3,000,000 would be liquidated, yielding $170,000,000,000 to be turned over to the United States Treasury.

2. From this fund, every family in the United States was to receive about $4,000 [or $5,000] to purchase a home, an automobile, and a radio. The estimated government expenditure for these services was $100,000,000,000.

122

3. All persons over sixty-five [or sixty] years of age were to receive pensions of $30 per month [or an adequate amount].

4. The minimum wage would be adjusted to provide a floor of $2,500 a year per worker, resulting in, among other things, a permanent increase in the purchasing power of the benefited group.

5. Hours of labor would be limited to balance industrial production with consumption and enable the worker to enjoy some of the conveniences of life.

6. The government would purchase and store agricultural surpluses in order to balance agricultural production with demand "according to the laws of God."

7. Cash payment of veterans' bonuses would begin immediately.

8. From the remainder of the Treasury fund, boys of proven ability, as determined by intelligence tests, were to receive a college education at government expense.[15]

The Roosevelt administration was irritated by the establishment of the Share-Our-Wealth movement and other Long challenges. It retaliated by encouraging the investigation of the election of a Long lieutenant, John Overton, to the Senate, giving federal patronage to anti-Long elements in Louisiana, and probing the tax returns of the Senator and his associates. Senator Long reacted by widening the breach between himself and the national administration. In April, 1934, the Louisianian declared his fundamental disagreement with the New Deal on agricultural, banking, and economy measures.[16] He began, early in 1935, his demands for a Senate investigation of James A. Farley, the Postmaster General and Democratic National Committee chairman.

With this attack on Farley, Home Owners Loan Corporation and Public Works Administration allotments to Louisiana were withheld by the federal government. This New Deal action occasioned a complete break between Roosevelt and Long. On the floor of the Senate, the Louisiana Senator openly denounced the administration, stating that under the New Deal the country was "headed just as straight to hell as a martin ever went to gourd." He asserted that his desire for a career in public life was not so great that it would cause him to "kneel to the crooks like men employed by Jim Farley. God send me to hell before I have to have patronage through that kind."[17] Two days later, Long spelled his thoughts out even more clearly and this time directed them at the President himself. In a radio address, the Louisianian declared that there was no more hope for the people in the policies of the Chief Executive, and he urged every American to join in support of the Share-Our-Wealth program. Long concluded by labeling the New Deal: "It is not Roosevelt or ruin, it is Roosevelt's ruin."[18] Less than two months later, Father Coughlin also made his formal declaration of war on the New Deal, crying that "you cannot have a new deal without a new deck." He charged that "every card dealt" by Roosevelt so far had been marked for "high finance" or "big business." The Detroit priest asserted that the New Deal represented "two years of economic failure."[19]

Long and Coughlin were answered by General Hugh S. Johnson, the former National Recovery

Administrator. Lashing out in a fiery manner, Johnson charged that "these two men are raging up and down this land preaching not construction, but destruction, not reform, but revolution, not peace, but a sword. I think we are dealing with a couple of Catilines and that it is high time for somebody to say so." Johnson also called upon Coughlin to quit the church.[20] Johnson's statement drew radio responses from both Long and Coughlin. Both of them repudiated the General's charges, while the Louisiana Senator described the General as being the "lead-off" man in a declaration of war by the administration.[21] Either at Roosevelt's behest or on his own authority, Johnson continued his campaign against Long and Coughlin by announcing that he was going to enlist "thinking Americans" into a force to combat them and their influence. Secretaries Ickes and Wallace, and Philippines High Commissioner Frank Murphy, with the President's knowledge, soon joined in the attack on Senator Long, with side blows aimed at Father Coughlin.[22] At this time other national political forces commenced their denunciation of the Long-Coughlin elements. The national executive committee of the Socialist party issued a warning to workingmen and agrarians, stating that a Long-Coughlin party would signal the end of organized farm and labor movements. Similar warnings were also presented by the Farmer-Labor Political Federation officials. The liberal-minded Methodist Federation for Social Service declared that Long, Coughlin, and Johnson were engaged in a race for fascist leadership. This organization described all three as being opponents of organized labor and charged that they were endeavoring to uphold an economic system which had been described by the General Conference of the Methodist Episcopal Church as being "unethical, unchristian and anti-social." The Methodist group later averred that Coughlin underpaid his workers and was using non-union printers. This was denied by the Detroit cleric.[23]

Coughlin did not make any threats of third-party action in the days immediately following his break with the President. Almost from the beginning, however, Huey Long started making references to such action. In the middle of March, 1935, Long threatened to bolt the Democratic party if Roosevelt should run for re-election. There also was talk of the Senator's entering Democratic presidential primaries in Georgia, North Dakota, Nebraska, and perhaps Mississippi, Alabama, and Arkansas in an attempt to capture that party. Then it was reported that he planned to use his following, in conjunction with those of Coughlin and Milo Reno, as the basis for a third-party movement. Late in April, 1935, the circle of political possibilities was completed when Senator Long pledged that he would join the GOP if it nominated Senator Borah for President; he asserted, however, that he would head a third-party ticket, if necessary, to defeat Roosevelt.[24]

Coughlin, like Long, conducted a strenuous speaking campaign on national issues, devoting a great deal of energy to building up the membership of his National Union for Social Justice. Within six months after its founding, the priest claimed eight and one-half million members for the organization. Although he kept his peace on Long, it is significant that his program and speeches were lauded by the Louisiana legislator. Coughlin, however, asserted that the National Union for Social Justice was not a political party and that he would not be a candidate for public office. This may have been a gesture to concentrate the Long-Coughlin-Reno strength on one possible candidate for the presidency in 1936. Coughlin evidently further developed his plans for using NUSJ, when, just prior to the July meeting of the Farmer-Labor Political Federation, he held that some sort of third party of the discontented was inevitable.[25] This was to mark the high point of the priest's public thinking on independent political action until he announced the formation of the Union party a year later.

Democratic party officials meanwhile became increasingly interested in the advances made by political independents. In the first half of 1935, a secret poll was conducted by the Democratic National Committee on Long's political popularity. James Farley reported that this canvass "disclosed, to our surprise, that [Long] might poll between 3,000,000 to 4,000,000 votes as the head of a third party." He revealed that the Louisiana Senator and his proposals were attracting balloting strength not just in Louisiana and adjacent states, but also in the manufactur-

ing and agricultural areas of the North. As it seemed
that Long was drawing support mainly from Democratic ranks, Farley concluded that the lawmaker, as
a third-party candidate, "might constitute a balance
of power in the 1936 election." In the summer of
1935, Farley, evidently disturbed at the indications
of the decline of Democratic strength, warned the
President that he had lost ground politically.
Whether Farley's statement that he personally "saw
no cause for alarm" was true or not, the administration attempted to deal more effectively with the
threats presented by the Long and Coughlin movements.[26] These endeavors apparently included a
"don't rock the boat" publicity campaign, and positive legislative action.

While the administration redoubled its efforts to
cope with the third-party danger, Long and Coughlin forged ahead in developing their respective personal organizations. The Louisiana legislator's plans
for national action had reached beyond unconnected,
random threats by August. At that time, Long revealed a fairly clear program for political activity in
1936. He would first attempt to gain the presidential
nomination of the Democratic party. Failing that,
Long asserted that he would bolt the party, although
he would try to secure the position of legal Democratic candidate in as many states as possible. He indicated that independent party action and a trading
of votes with the Republicans might be feasible. The
goals of his strategy, in order of their priority, were:
(1) to defeat any Roosevelt bid for re-election; (2)

128

to obtain the implementation of the Share-Our-
Wealth program; and (3) to gain election as President.[27]

The Long threat to the New Deal, of course,
never materialized *per se*. On the morning of September 10, 1935, Senator Long died of bullet wounds
received at the hands of Dr. Carl Weiss, Jr. The chief
organizer of the Share-Our-Wealth movement, the
Rev. Gerald L. K. Smith, took steps to try to forestall
the disintegration of the national following that
Long had developed. He jumped into the news by
implying, in the name of the "10,000,000 members"
of the Share-Our-Wealth Society of America, that
Long had really been the victim of the national administration's opposition. Smith demanded that the
President launch an impartial investigation of the
assassination to clear the New Deal of any suspicion
of complicity in the Louisiana Senator's death.
Long's lieutenant later charged that the absence of a
suitable federal investigation into the assassination
implicated the administration. On that basis, Smith
tried to conserve the political strength of the Share-
Our-Wealth clubs.[28]

Thus, with the death of Huey Long, one of the
most controversial political figures of the 1930's and
1940's was catapulted from virtual obscurity to become the American most often characterized as the
leading native fascist. Lacking the rustic charm, at
least the suggestion of social consciousness, and the
adeptness at organization and political appeal
possessed by Long, Smith was unable to prevent the

disintegration of most of the Share-Our-Wealth movement. Smith's appeal to "Longolatry" was even less effective in preventing Long's Louisiana machine from co-operating with the national administration.[29] As a result, Smith "was all titivated up and hadn't any place to go." But he was to keep seeking until he found a place, first in the Townsend movement as Townsend's assistant and then in the Union party. In his organizational wanderings, Smith developed a rather interesting interpretation of Long's program and methods. He described Long's "sainted" Louisiana regime as being like "the dictatorship of the surgical theater. After all, the surgeon is put in charge because he knows. The nurses and assistants therefore defer to him, not because they are servile, but because they believe in the surgeon and realize that he is working for the welfare of the patient." From this relatively subdued observation, Smith moved to more startling ejaculations: "We're too soft and flabby. There are more lazy men in the country today than ever before in its history. That's why we have such lousy government. The lowest form of animal life in this country is the United States Congress." One of his favorite slogans was that "politics is prostitution." Opposed to any form of public ownership—even police and fire department services—and being an avowed anti-Semite, the Rev. Mr. Smith defined "true Americanism" as, first, to "preserve the sacred right of private property; second, help to uphold the Constitution; third, glorify the American flag; and lastly, drive the Com-

munists out of the country."[30] It was hard for most
of the American citizenry to see how these statements
could, on the whole, square with Long's ideas. It
seemed that Smith, as much if not more than those
politicians who had inherited Long's Louisiana machine, was invoking his name to cover up his own
ideas and goals, while essentially discarding Long's
program. Whether Smith's co-operation with
Coughlin, Lemke, and Townsend in the Union
party added anything to that movement is questionable. One cannot doubt, however, that many of the
farmer-laborites of the Midwest were scared away by
Smith's campaign statements.

With the coast-to-coast extension of Father
Coughlin's broadcasts in the fall of 1935, and the establishment of the NUSJ newspaper, *Social Justice,*
in March, 1936, many more people were brought
into contact with the priest and his criticisms of the
New Deal.[31] Early in his 1935-1936 radio series,
Coughlin served notice on behalf of the National
Union for Social Justice that the "open hunting
season for members of Congress is on." He also proclaimed to the "Asiatic Communists, to the extreme
socialists, to the European Fascists and plutocratic
money manufacturers that this is the United States
and that we, its citizens, will tolerate no upstart and
no group of upstarts who will attempt to claim for
themselves the regency of our nation."[32] His strong
indictments of Congress and the nation's bankers
throughout the series were typified by the following
passage:

Oftentimes there is as little distinction between a Democrat and a Republican member of Congress as there was between two worms gnawing on one apple. Exploitation of the inarticulate people continued until wealth was concentrated in the hands of a few. The Constitution of the United States was degraded while Congress after Congress supported the private coinage and fixation of money. Consistently they permitted profits to pile up prodigiously for the owners of industry in a machine age when the laborer was being paid less and when his toil was wanted less. Consistently they forced the farmers of the nation, at least since 1920, to operate at a loss. Instead of supplying the country with honest American credit, Congress has cooperated with the privately owned Federal Reserve bankers, permitting them to create credit out of nothing while the same Congress expects us and future generations to repay these bankers with currency money that does not exist.[33]

Shifting his attack to the executive branch of government, Coughlin charged that "generally speaking, the New Deal is nothing more than a skilled nurse attempting, through the administration of opiates, to restore health to the body of plutocracy."[34] The Detroit cleric contended that the only difference between the Republicans and the Democrats was that the latter helped the poor a bit. He averred, however, that regardless of this, whichever organization won the 1936 elections, the American Liberty League would actually be the winner. Coughlin condemned the New Deal for paying a "slave-wage" to public works employees, while continuing to pay standard interest and profits to the banking and manufacturing interests which were co-operating with the government. When all the evidence was studied, he felt

that no one could disagree with his characterization
of the New Deal: "While its golden head enunciates
the splendid program of Christian justice, its feet of
sordid clay are mired, one in the red mud of Soviet
communism, and the other, in the stinking cesspool
of pagan plutocracy."[35]

As for the world situation, the 1935-1936 radio
broadcasts cautioned that British bankers were pre-
paring to plunge the United States into another
world war. Coughlin felt that, however, there was a
chance that the war might be postponed until 1937.
Condemning the League of Nations as "a nameless,
illegitimate child which was cradled in the adulter-
ous bed of the Treaty of Versailles," he called for
the following diplomatic policy for America: "No
entanglements with foreign nations. . . . No participation in sanctions against either England or Ethi-
opia or Italy. . . . No credit to warring nations because credit has been abused and our debts have
been repudiated. . . . We stand for an uncompromising and permanent declaration of our neutrality."
This foreign policy was neatly summed up in the
priest's demand of "America for the Americans."[36]
Thus, Coughlin's radio lecture series attacked bankers, the capitalist system, collective security, Communism, the American Liberty League, the New
Deal, and occasionally Fascism or Nazism. Coughlin
was, however, generous in his praise of the goals of
NUSJ. These goals were epitomized as being necessary to the establishment of a system wherein future
wealth would be more equitably distributed. The

National Union was to serve the purpose of co-ordi-
nating and solidifying the scattered forces of national
interest upon a program that was "socially just for
all," so that candidates for public office would have
no difficulty in knowing the people's will.[37]

A' has been seen, the radio priest's attacks caused
a good deal of concern to the New Deal administration. It was easy enough for New Deal spokesmen to
counterattack Long and even Smith, but when it
came to Coughlin political expediency dictated that
another policy be followed. The priest's platform
and lectures were so complex and all-inclusive in
their condemnation of the current system that it
was difficult to answer his charges. And the same
problem presented itself in trying to undercut his
complaints through positive legislative and admin-
istrative action. Moreover, his status as a clergyman
made the problem a ticklish one; it was feared that
the denunciation of a Roman Catholic priest by a
predominantly Protestant government would result
in accusations of Ku Kluxism and religious persecution. The President tried to avoid giving direct attention to Coughlin. James Farley tells us that in a
May, 1935, meeting of ranking Democratic leaders,
Roosevelt indicated that great harm had been done
"in the speech [Secretary Ickes] made at Philadelphia. . . . I had no objections to what he said about
Long or Townsend, but his reference to Father
Coughlin was very unwise."[38] Defense of the New
Deal and criticism of Coughlin, however, came during 1935 from some of the less well-known members

of the American Catholic clergy. As the Coughlin attacks increased in intensity late in the year and as it became more apparent that NUSJ might be used as more than a debating society, the first widely publicized rebuke of the priest was issued by a major leader of the church. At that time, the Archbishop of Chicago, George Cardinal Mundelein, made one of his infrequent public political statements in order to praise the fairness and courage of Roosevelt. The Cardinal, in a radio speech delivered at the University of Notre Dame, then denounced those who would drag the church into the American political arena.[39] After Cardinal Mundelein's pronouncement, church criticism of Coughlin became more frequent, although it did not receive the publicity given Coughlin until during the presidential campaign of 1936.

Meanwhile, late in 1935, another protest movement started to share the political headlines. This was the Townsend Old Age Pension Group. Fathered by a retired physician, Dr. Francis E. Townsend, the movement was designed to gain not only economic security for the aged but prosperity for the nation. In brief, Townsend proposed that the federal government should distribute $200 a month to every American citizen of good character, not gainfully employed, who was over sixty years of age. The recipients would have been required to spend the money within the United States or its dependencies within a month after receipt. It was estimated by Townsend that this plan would add $19,200,000,000 to the purchasing power of the country every year and that this sum would give the necessary "big push" to stimulate our economy to prosperity. The money to finance the pensions was to be raised by a federal stamp tax of 2 per cent or less on every business transaction.[40] Originally, Townsend's followers talked in terms of using only pressure-group methods to gain their goal. But as the movement gained strength and encountered increasing resistance, its membership tended to think in terms of direct political action. Townsend himself was not enthusiastic about the benefits that might be conferred upon his group by this means. Eventually, however, he was carried into the area of direct political action by the urgings of his more vocal followers and by pleas from Coughlin's representatives.

Although the Townsend movement had been active and growing in importance since its formation on New Year's Day, 1934, President Roosevelt was evidently not aware of its importance until late in the summer of 1935. At that time a most forceful letter by Dr. Stanley High was called to his attention. High wrote that in every area in the West which he had visited on a fact-finding tour, the most dynamic movement in operation was the Townsend group. He reported that at least a dozen seasoned political observers had told him that by 1936, the Townsend-ites would have control of the political balance of power in their Congressional districts. High further stated that Townsend was apparently angered at not being able to secure an interview with the President.

He also commented that it was known that the physician had had long conversations with Herbert Hoover, who was then considered to be a candidate for the Republican presidential nomination. High ventured the opinion that the biggest political mistake in 1936 would be made by those who ignored the Townsend movement. Several letters from prominent Democrats, which the President presumably saw either condensed or in full, further revealed anxiety about the lack of administration action to cope with the Townsend group. One Congressman, Martin F. Smith of Washington, indicated to James Farley that he was going to take matters into his own hands in regard to Townsend. Representative Smith wrote that he planned to address the 1935 Townsend Convention in an endeavor to hold the nation's aged in line for the Democrats. He asserted that the Republicans were courting the Townsend people and that the Democrats had to pay attention to an organization which had millions of loyal members. Later, the Chief Executive got in touch with the Social Security Board to find out how it planned to offset the political appeal of the Townsend Plan. The Board chairman, John G. Winant, replied that the Board was cognizant of the problem of Townsendism and that it was endeavoring to devise a program of public information in regard to Social Security. Winant averred that such a program should be positive in nature rather than an attempt to discredit other plans and programs.[41] Of course, the Social Security Act which was signed in August, 1935, seemed unsatisfactory to the Townsendites and other old-age groups. It did not cover even a majority of Americans and one had to be working to hope ever to gain maximum benefits from it. In addition, the cash benefits, which seemed insultingly low to older people, were not to be paid at the earliest until 1937.[42]

Evidently the rising interest of the administration failed to stem the ardor of the Townsendites. Some 12,000 people representing 5,000 clubs met in a national convention in Chicago in December, 1935. This convention approved a resolution calling for the entry of presidential and Congressional candidates by the Townsendites in the 1936 elections. It was reported that the convention's spokesmen expected they could control from seven to fifteen million votes and would elect 150 Congressmen. Dr. Townsend, however, did not agree with the convention's position. He explained that the convention resolution did not necessarily point to third-party action. Rather, he felt that his organization's energies should be directed toward endorsing approved nominees of the two old parties, in order to give these groups a chance to solve the problems of the aged. Within a week after the convention, the physician dramatically announced his support of the candidacy of a Republican Plan backer in a by-election in the third Michigan Congressional district. This candidate, V. W. Main, was elected by a two-to-one majority. Townsend accepted a good deal of the credit for Main's victory.[43] The Republican party, however, proved to be as indifferent to the Townsend Plan as the Democratic party. Late in March, 1936, Townsend asserted that if his plan continued to receive a cool reception from the two major parties, "a third party, composed exclusively of Townsend Plan followers, will be formulated, with the avowed purpose of shelving both Democrat and Republican parties perpetually." Bitterly, the physician, commenting upon the friendly overtures made by Senator Borah toward the nation's elder citizens and "their Plan," remarked that Borah was "the only one to show sympathetic attitude toward our movement."[44]

Another factor that tended to drive Townsend over into the third-party camp was the investigation of possible fiscal fraud in the operation of the Townsend organization by a House subcommittee headed by Representative C. Jasper Bell of Missouri. After preliminary investigations, Congressman Bell forthrightly labeled the Plan a hoax upon the old people of the country. Dr. Townsend intemperately lashed out at the subcommittee several times; e.g., "The only hoax I know of in relation to the Townsend Plan is the Bell investigating committee." These sharp retorts, coupled with the refusal of the physician and two of his aides to co-operate with the investigators, resulted in the passage, 271-41, of a House resolution calling for their trial on the charge of contempt of Congress.[45] Letters from Townsend clubs and individual followers flooded Congress and the White House protesting this action. Typical of the complaints was that sent by Townsend Club

139

13, Spokane, Washington: "The Malicious Attack made upon the most Humanitarian Plan ever placed before our American People is hardly believable. Thank God, we have the ballot next November to express our feelings toward those men who dare to perpetrate such a dastardly deed as is now on Record."[46] It was indicated by Townsend and Gerald L. K. Smith that the investigation was planned by the administration as a method of discrediting Townsend and his plan. Smith stated that Farley was driving Townsend, Coughlin, and himself to "congeal under a leadership with guts" in order to cope with the New Dealers. *Social Justice,* seconding Smith in a more genteel fashion, further commented: "While the principles of the Townsend Plan are most beneficial, it is our conviction that such reform cannot be expected to meet with any degree of success under our present economic conditions. The aims that the Townsend Clubs are striving to obtain are automatically included in the sixteen principles of the National Union for Social Justice."[47]

Whether the Congressional investigation of the Townsend movement inspired the specific action which gave birth to the Union party can only be a matter of conjecture. Obviously, however, after the Bell investigation, Coughlin, Townsend, and Smith increased the fury of their attacks upon the government. Moreover, since the farmer-labor party movement had collapsed in May, the most important potential competitor in the third-party field had been removed. This perhaps convinced the third-party ad-

140

vocates in the Smith, Coughlin, and Townsend groups that June was the time to strike for a new party. The National Union for Social Justice had already entered into the 1936 political struggle by endorsing Congressional candidates in various parts of the nation. In May, for example, twenty-five NUSJ endorsees obtained Democratic or Republican nominations in Pennsylvania and Ohio.[48] Father Coughlin took the initiative in the middle of June, and advised the nation of the formation of a united political front of the National Union for Social Justice, the Share-Our-Wealth Society, the Townsend movement, and the Lemkeites. (This latter designation presumably referred to the agrarian admirers of Congressman William Lemke of North Dakota, who had been increasingly critical of the administration's agricultural and fiscal policies; Lemke's followers included remnants of the Nonpartisan League, of which he had been a leader.) The Detroit priest stated that the candidate representative of their union would be announced within a week.[49] Representative Kvale of Minnesota expressed the sentiment of most Farmer-Laborites when he declared that Coughlin's suggestion for a third party of radicals "seems ill-timed and the proposed organization impracticable." Representative Amlie, speaking for the radical wing of the Wisconsin Progressive party, stated that the Coughlin united front could accomplish but little without the support of labor, the absence of which was noticeably apparent in the proposed new party. Perhaps the strangest thing in the evolution of the new party was that Townsend and Smith, the titular leaders of two of the key movements which Coughlin had announced to be sponsors of the new united front, immediately denied any political alliance with NUSJ and the Lemke followers for action in the 1936 campaign.[50]

On June 19, in a speech by Father Coughlin over the Columbia Broadcasting System, the birth of the new Union party was formally announced. In justifying the establishment of the new party, Coughlin declared that Americans must be saved from "sham":

Neither Old Dealer nor New Dealer, it appears, has courage to assail the international bankers, the Federal Reserve bankers. In common, both the Republicans and the Democrats uphold the old money philosophy, as their convention bands harmoniously strike up the tune of "Semper Fidelis," everlastingly faithful to Wall Street, to the underwriters of the World War, to the exploiters of the poor, to the merchants of death and misery. . . . I refuse to remain in the mud and slime of needless poverty, hemmed in by the barbed wire entanglements of want in the midst of plenty, and a target for the sharp shooters of high finance.

The priest then proclaimed Representative Lemke and Thomas C. O'Brien, former Suffolk County, Massachusetts, district attorney, to be, respectively, the presidential and vice-presidential nominees of the new party.[51] In a document designed to contain the essence of the political, economic, and social demands of the Townsend, Coughlin, Smith, and Lemke groups, the following platform was outlined: (1) American self-containment and self-sustainment, with a complete disavowal of foreign entanglements; (2) complete Congressional control of coinage, credit, and money-value through a central bank of issue; (3) retirement of all tax-exempt, interest-bearing bonds and certificates, and government refinancing of farm and home mortagages; (4) Congressional assurance of a living annual wage; (5) Congressional guarantee of production at a profit for farmers; (6) Congressional guarantee of reasonable and decent security for the aged; (7) Congressional protection of our agricultural, industrial, and commercial markets from the manipulation of foreign moneys and those foreign imports produced at less than a living wage; (8) Congressional provision for an adequate and perfect defense from foreign aggression, and disavowal of the use of American armed forces in foreign lands or waters, with conscription of wealth as well as of men in case of war; (9) total extension of the merit system to appointive government positions; (10) "ruthless eradication of bureaucracies"; (11) increased public-works programs, especially in the area of conservation, at the prevailing wage; (12) decentralization of economic monopolies to protect small business; (13) elimination of unnecessary taxation, and allegiance to the principle that the "human rights of the masses take precedence over the financial rights of the classes"; (14) Congressional limitation of annual net incomes and inheritances by taxation; and (15) Congressional provision of conditions that will enable our school and college graduates to obtain jobs.[52]

In reacting to the Lemke candidacy, we find that Gerald L. K. Smith, with characteristic bluntness, was not concerned with Lemke's qualifications or with the party's platform. Smith wanted to know what the Representative would offer him for his support. This bartering process did not seem to dampen Lemke's enthusiasm. The North Dakota Congressman stated that his goal was not to split the vote of either major party, but was to become President. "I will defeat both of my closest competitors—Roosevelt and Landon." Lemke asserted that the people, being sufficiently informed of the state of affairs, "no longer believe them nor do they have confidence in either of these parties. They demand Fair Play and not a New Deal or a New Shuffle." More specifically, he predicted that he would carry all of New England, most of the Middle West, the extreme West, and Pennsylvania. Coughlin predicted that 85 per cent of the NUSJ's members would cast their votes for Lemke, although formal endorsement of the Union party nominee would have to wait until the August convention of NUSJ. Both men stated that they hoped the Townsend convention would endorse Lemke.[53] The Townsend movement never officially sponsored the Union party, for fear that its direct endorsement would "complicate the issues." Dr. Townsend, however, did campaign for Representative Lemke and reminded his followers that the Congressman was their only friend among the 1936 crop of presidential aspirants.[54] The president of the National Farmers' Union asserted that Lemke would

144

have the support of that organization's members in large measure. "General" Coxey withdrew his independent presidential candidacy in order to throw his support to the North Dakotan.[55] In the national convention of the Farm Holiday Association, the matter of endorsing Lemke was fought to a stalemate. Five state Holiday Association presidents, however, announced their refusal to abide by this failure to act, and asserted that they were going to form a "real" farmers' organization. Incidentally, this secession movement was directed by Representative Usher L. Burdick of North Dakota, who was serving as Lemke's campaign manager. This group charged that Communists had gained complete control of the Farm Holiday meeting.[56]

The *New York Times* reported that some Democratic leaders feared the loss of North Dakota, South Dakota, Montana, and Minnesota, owing to Lemke's candidacy, and that top-level Democratic conferences were being held to assess the ramifications of the Union party's formation.[57] In July, however, President Roosevelt, in a letter to Vice President Garner, wrote that "curiously enough, I don't think the Lemke ticket will cut into our vote any more than it will into the Republican vote."[58] Another problem arose to worry the New Deal Democrats at this time. Since August, 1935, rumors had been circulating to the effect that some conservative Democratic leaders would bolt their party in protest against Roosevelt's policies. Two days after the formation of the Union party, it was announced that Alfred Smith, former

Secretary of State Bainbridge Colby, ex-Governor Joseph B. Ely of Massachusetts, and ex-Senator James A. Reed had urged the delegates to the Democratic convention to repudiate the New Deal. They also asked that "some genuine Democrat" be substituted for Roosevelt on the ticket. After the President's renomination in July, Ely, Reed and some other prominent Democrats proclaimed their support of Landon. Alfred Smith declared for the Republican presidential candidate in October.[59]

The more orthodox segments of the nation's radicals and progressives subjected the new party to a rigid baptism of fire. Earl Browder charged that "the self-styled 'Union Party,' secretly manufactured in the laboratory of Coughlin and Lemke and sprung upon the world full-grown, bears all the earmarks of a Hearst-Landon-Liberty League intrigue. . . . [Lemke's] program is a typical half-fascist hodgepodge of radical sounding phrases without any definite commitment on a single concrete issue." Norman Thomas stated that "it is doubtful if this Union party—a union of two and a half Messiahs plus some neo-Populists—will be permanent. But it is a portent. There is about its appearance and program much that smacks of early Fascism in Europe." Declaring the claims of the Union party sponsors to five to fifteen million votes "absurd," the *Nation* described the party as being a successful attempt "to combine under one banner all the major crackpot movements America has seen in the past decade." The *New Republic* dismissed the new movement as being "definitely fascistic." Campaigning on behalf of farmer-labor Congressional candidates, Howard Y. Williams called the Lemke candidacy a tragic mistake and warned that it would split the progressive vote. Williams concluded, on the basis of his intimate knowledge of progressive-radical circles, that there was little grass roots support behind the Union party. *Common Sense* probably described well the feeling of most progressives in the 1936 election: "Where do we stand? We confess to being without conviction in the matter of the presidential election. We feel not unlike little boys who ponder the philosophical question, Do you prefer castor oil or going to the dentist?" The magazine rejected the Republicans as completely negativistic, the Communists as dictatorial, and the Socialists as too divided to be able to accomplish anything. As for the Union party, its sponsors were referred to as "fascists," "demagogues," "Jew baiters," "crackpots," and "nonentities."[60]

In launching the Union party campaign, Father Coughlin, in an address over the Columbia Broadcasting System, asserted that the Lemke-O'Brien candidacy was perfectly representative of the American people. He pointed out that Protestant Lemke stood for Western, agricultural, and intelligent Republican protest to the New Deal, while his Catholic running-mate represented the true thinking of Democrats, the East, and Labor (O'Brien was employed as a lawyer for the Brotherhood of Railway Trainmen). Behind this ticket, the priest claimed, "will rally agriculture, labor, the disappointed Re-

147

publicans and the outraged Democrats, the independent merchant and industrialist, and every lover of liberty who desires to eradicate the cancerous growths from decadent capitalism and avoid the treacherous pitfalls of red communism."[61] Soon after the appearance of this statement, Coughlin announced that he was immediately undertaking an organizational and speaking tour in the East and the Middle West. At the outset of that trip, *Social Justice* claimed that the National Union for Social Justice would be able to deliver five million votes to Lemke. Later on in the campaign, however, the NUSJ newspaper estimated that Lemke would attract only 8 per cent of the total vote, which, it was claimed, would throw the election to the House of Representatives and, therefore, would lead to a free-for-all battle for the presidency.[62]

As has been previously indicated, personalities made for the most significant difference between the Union party and other progressive-radical movements. It was, therefore, no surprise that the party's platform, whatever its merit, was not really subjected to scrutiny or discussion. The attention the party received was focused on its leaders; this, of course, was disadvantageous to the organization in view of the dramatic and extreme statements made by some of them. Certainly, there was a good deal of adverse reaction to Coughlin's alleged Jew-baiting. Statements like the following alarmed radicals throughout the nation: "I am not asking the Jews of the United States to accept Christianity and all of its beliefs but,

148

since their system of a tooth for a tooth and an eye for an eye has failed, that they accept Christ's principle of brotherhood."[63] Furthermore, many resented Coughlin's attempts to invest the Union party with sole possession of patriotism and piety. Typical of these efforts was his statement that "this is not a question of electing Landon or of ousting Roosevelt. This is a question of fighting to the last drop of our political blood and with the last ounce of strength of our love of liberty"; or his radio speech of September 19, in which he declared: "The issue is not Roosevelt or Landon or Lemke; it is Christianity or chaos; Americanism or Communism."[64] Smith entered the campaign with even less caution of tongue than Coughlin, and the two of them together far outweighed the more moderate and temperate statements made by Lemke and Townsend in the 1936 campaign. Another political blunder was made by the Union forces when Lemke allowed Coughlin's newspaper, *Social Justice,* to give him the campaign nickname of "Liberty Bell Bill." Almost every major party representative, who condescended to take notice of the North Dakotan's candidacy, referred to the fact that the Liberty Bell is cracked and hinted that so perhaps was Lemke.[65]

The progressives of the nation seemed to have been in large part disturbed by the course of political developments in 1936. Of course, they did not agree completely with the President, but they felt that his program was better than those presented by any other candidate. Surveying their actions and thought,

149

one may conclude that they recognized three men-
aces: (1) the Landon candidacy as supported by the
Liberty League; (2) the opposition and the revolt of
the conservatives within the Democratic party; and
(3) Lemke's Union party campaign. As a result of
these fears, three significant progressive-liberal movements arose to protect the Roosevelt program. These
three groups included some people who were
squarely behind the New Deal and others, like the
progressives, who felt that half a loaf—or even
crumbs—was preferable to no bread at all. The first
of these three was a shadowy anti-Coughlin movement within the Catholic Church. Many Catholics
agreed with Coughlin that there was a pressing need
for an adequate standard of living for the country's
people and that there was great need for world peace,
but they could not agree that the elimination of
Roosevelt and the repudiation of the idea of world
co-operation would secure these results. Therefore,
soon after the formation of the Union party, certain
members of the Catholic Church began to take steps
to combat Coughlin. The Rev. Maurice S. Sheehy,
Assistant to the Rector of the Catholic University
of America, wrote the President a letter which was
indicative of Catholic opposition to Coughlin.
Father Sheehy stated that four bishops, three mon-
signori, and two priests had met in New York to
formulate a plan of action to offset Coughlin's attacks on the President. They agreed that the President should not take cognizance of the Detroit
priest's attacks but that Roosevelt should allow his

150

friends within the church to defend him. Neither the names of the clergymen involved in this meeting nor the methods to which the group addressed itself were revealed.[66] The fact that the meeting occurred, however, and the events that followed showed that prominent churchmen were determined that Coughlin should meet with organized resistance. The newspapers of the period were filled with the debate within the church regarding Coughlin. Bishop Mahoney of Sioux Falls, South Dakota, to whom Coughlin was a "clerical vulgarian," was quite active in denouncing the head of NUSJ. Bishop Joseph Schrembs of Cleveland asserted that a priest has the right to discuss political and social issues, but that it is unwise for a clergyman to take a prominent part in a political campaign. After Coughlin's famous statements that Roosevelt was a "dictator" and an "anti-God," the Archbishop of Cincinnati and the Vatican newspaper, *Osservatore Romano,* rebuked the Detroit priest unequivocally.[67] The most outspoken defender of the President in the Catholic Church, Monsignor John A. Ryan of the Catholic University of America, continually clashed with Coughlin, charging him with misinterpreting and misquoting papal encyclicals. Father Coughlin replied usually by referring to Monsignor Ryan as the "Right Reverend New Dealer."[68] Coughlin, of course, had his champions among the clergy and laity of the Catholic Church. He was defended in his actions—at least as to his rights, if not as to substance—by his immediate superior, Bishop Gallagher of Detroit. Many prominent Catholic laymen, including Congressmen John P. Higgins, Arthur D. Healey, and Joseph E. Casey of Massachusetts, repudiated Roosevelt to support the radio priest.[69] And so, throughout the summer and fall of 1936, the battle raged within the church. It is impossible to measure the effect of this struggle upon interested Catholics and non-Catholics, but perhaps the ignominious failure of the Lemke-O'-Brien ticket at the polls reflected the strength of Coughlin's opponents within the church.

The second organization fighting for Roosevelt, of which mention has already been made, was Labor's Non-Partisan League. This organization was founded in April, 1936, by George L. Berry, president of the Printing Pressmen's Union, Sidney Hillman, president of the Amalgamated Clothing Workers, and John L. Lewis, president of the United Mine Workers, with the goal of organizing "as an instrumentality of the furtherance of liberalism in the United States."[70] The League pledged itself to co-operate with progressives to gain common goals. It was implied that this was to be accomplished by their joint support of Roosevelt in 1936, and then by their joining hands in the establishment of a new progressive-radical party after the election. In fact, the formation of the American Labor party in New York during 1936 by the League and the Social Democratic Federation—the right-wing splinter from the Socialist party—was based on these premises.[71] Labor's Non-Partisan League represented an eventually successful attempt at compromise between the advocates of nonpartisanship and the labor-party sentiment within the labor movement. As such, the organization was to be "a propaganda league which continued to adhere to Gompers' dictum, 'Reward your friends, punish your enemies,' but did it no longer through platonic words and nice pronouncements but through a well-oiled and organized political machine." Some idea of Labor's Non-Partisan League's 1936 campaign activities can be gained from Sidney Lens' description:

> It spent almost a million dollars and considerable energy. In Ohio the league conducted 344 political rallies, sent 70 speakers almost daily to talk to union meetings and other groups, and broadcast a half-hour program in five large cities for thirty days prior to the election. A national radio broadcast from Reno to New York City was also beamed to workers every day for a month before the balloting. Meetings, circulars, pamphlets, and other activity unquestionably brought many votes to the Roosevelt column. In Chicago the league held 109 rallies and visited every single ward. The most intense and sustained activity, however, was in Pennsylvania. A total of some 35,000 union officials were enlisted in the drive to keep Roosevelt in the White House.[72]

There is little doubt that Labor's Non-Partisan League, by aiding in effectively marshaling labor into the President's camp, contributed significantly in undercutting whatever appeal the Union party might have had for workingmen.

The third important organization which entered into the battle to combat Lemke, Landon, and the conservative Democrats, was the Progressive National Committee Supporting Franklin D. Roosevelt or President. Born of a meeting of progressives in Chicago, September 11, 1936, the Progressive National Committee endeavored to deliver the nation's independent voters to Roosevelt in 1936. A partial list of the Committee's sponsors in that meeting indicates its diversified appeal: Representative Thomas Amlie, Farmer-Labor Governor Elmer Benson (Floyd Olson's successor as the chief executive of Minnesota), Senator Hugo Black, Senator Edward Costigan, Sidney Hillman, Robert and Philip La Follette, Fiorello La Guardia, John L. Lewis, Maury Maverick, George Norris, Lewis Schwellenbach, and Frank P. Walsh. Senators La Follette, Norris, and Costigan were elected, incidentally, as Chairman, Honorary Chairman, and Honorary Vice Chairman, respectively, of the Committee. Proclaiming its solid support of the President's campaign, the new organization issued the following statement, which was largely aimed at the Union party:

Political realignments cannot be made to order. Nor can they be built overnight to last. The foundations must be right. The roof cannot be put on before the underpinning is in, otherwise there is likely to be disaster for the whole enterprise.

Realignment is rapidly advancing. Reactionaries are united behind the Republican nominee. They know they cannot win against united progressives. Hence they hope to win by dividing progressives. Once attaining power they propose to keep it by whatever ruthless means are necessary.

In this critical situation division of liberals has only one result and that is direct support for reaction. Progressives, regardless of good motives, who aid in dividing those opposed to reaction, must share responsibility for the result.

An unbiased examination of the field makes it unmistakably clear that the next President of the United States will be Roosevelt or Landon. In this campaign there is therefore only one choice for American Progressives.[73]

Soon after the formation of the Progressive National Committee, it was announced that it would co-operate closely with Labor's Non-Partisan League during the election campaign so that "ammunition" might not be wasted. As proof of their alliance, the organizations jointly sponsored, beginning September 28, a five-week nightly series of radio programs to be broadcast over the Columbia Broadcasting System "appealing to all progressives to unite in support of Mr. Roosevelt."[74] The Committee also sponsored innumerable rallies and speaking campaigns, and circulated probably a million lots of literature on behalf of Roosevelt and his program.[75]

The business-like manner in which the independent and Democratic supporters of Roosevelt conducted their campaigns, and the many political mistakes made by Coughlin, Smith, Lemke, and Townsend, spelled the collapse of the Union party. Within a few weeks after its formation, it started on the downgrade, and by October it was fairly obvious that the party would fall far short of its claims of strength. Douglas Aikman observed that Lemke's political incapacity and the lack of enthusiasm generated by him, the labeling of Roosevelt as an "anti-God" and a Communist, and the advocacy of the use of bullets against Communism by Coughlin and Smith had alienated millions of potential Union

155

party supporters. Aikman predicted, in the middle of October, that Lemke would receive at most a million and a half votes as compared with the three and a half million conservatively prophesied in June. The *New York Times,* in an editorial written a week before the balloting, opined that the Union party was serving not to injure the New Deal strength, as was predicted earlier, but rather was detracting from Landon's power of appeal.[76]

On going to the polls, the American people over-whelmingly supported Roosevelt, gave a sharp slap to the Republicans, and virtually ignored the Lemke candidacy. The North Dakota Congressman received 882,479 votes out of over 45,000,000 cast, less than 2 per cent of the total. An analysis of Lemke's voting support has shown that he received his ballots in areas which had a high percentage of German, Catholic, and old-age voters.[77] The party did not elect any of its gubernatorial nominees, and no Union party Congressional candidate received election as a Unionist. Incidentally, Lemke ran success-fully for re-election to Congress as a Republican and a Unionist. Receiving votes in thirty-four states, the North Dakotan ran under several banners, including Union, Royal Oak, Union Progressive, Third Party, and National Union for Social Justice. Lemke's best showing was made in his home state, where he re-ceived about one out of every eight ballots cast.[78] While the Union party was not electorally successful, it did accomplish two things. It helped to unite the bulk of progressives in support of Roosevelt even if only for a brief moment. Moreover, as the *Superior Evening Telegram* observed, the election "served notice that the American people want no part of the things for which [Huey] Long stood. Everyone connected with him was repudiated. The idea of strong-arm stuff in American politics took as severe a beating as the most ardent lover of democracy could wish."[79]

Chapter VI
THE LAST CHANCE

The failures of the Farmer-Labor and Union movements had not killed third-party sentiment in the United States. While Roosevelt's electoral victory was overwhelming, many potential third-party advocates felt that they had played an indispensable role in the President's triumph. In addition, they had scored important election victories in their own right. In Minnesota, Farmer-Laborite Elmer Benson attracted a record-breaking vote and plurality in the gubernatorial contest, polling almost 700,000 votes; in Wisconsin, Governor Philip La Follette garnered almost 600,000 ballots in his successful campaign for re-election. *Common Sense* proclaimed that "already there are signs . . . that they are taking their own overwhelming independent victory of November 3rd as indication that the Farmer Labor and Progressive movements have a greater future than ever."[1] Governor La Follette's executive secretary wrote to a friend that the prospects for the development of a new national party looked splendid. Citing increased co-operation between the Minnesota and Wisconsin movements, he predicted that the next step toward a new party would be to establish a national organization to lay the basis for such a party in the various states.[2] Newly elected Farmer-Laborite Senator Ernest Lundeen, a perennial third-party proponent, announced that the Farmer-Labor Service Bureau, which had been maintained in his House of Representatives offices for four years, had been removed to larger quarters in Washington in January, 1937. Senator Lundeen offered the services of the bureau to all who were interested in the establishment of a new national party. In the summer of 1937, the Minnesota Farmer-Labor Association Executive Committee announced that progress had been made toward holding a joint meeting of committees representing farmer-labor forces in Minnesota and Wisconsin.[3] During 1937 and 1938 Henry G. Teigan (now a Representative in Congress), Farmer-Labor Executive Secretary Harold Peterson, and Howard Y. Williams, among others, also devoted a good deal of time on behalf of the Minnesota Farmer-Labor party to the organization of third-party groups in a number of states.

The American Labor party, born in 1936 of cooperation between Labor's Non-Partisan League and the Social Democratic Federation, seemed also to be making substantial progress. Roosevelt had received 274,924 votes under its banners in 1936, whereas the party contributed almost 500,000 ballots—the margin of victory—to Mayor Fiorello La Guardia's 1937 election campaign. Moreover, the American Labor party was able to elect five of its members to the New York City Council. Calling for low-cost housing, taxation based upon the capacity to pay, protection of constitutionally guaranteed civil liberties, broader social security coverage, and the maintenance of peace, this "anti-fascist" group announced that it looked forward to a "new political

159

alignment." ALP leaders, in conjunction with Mayor La Guardia and Acting Minnesota Governor Hjalmar Petersen, had warned late in the 1936 campaign that "there may be a national Farmer-Labor party in 1940."[4] Labor's Non-Partisan League claimed to have recruited or held millions of voters for Roosevelt in 1936. Moving to expand its strength, the League announced after the election that it was increasing its local political and lobbying organizations. League leaders frequently declared that there would be a political realignment by 1940; they stated that this might take the form of a new national party if the Democratic party failed to become thoroughly liberal.[5] Soon after the 1936 campaign, Clarence Senior, the executive secretary of the Socialist party, expressed the hope that Labor's Non-Partisan League would take the initiative in forming a national farmer-labor party. The Socialist party national executive committee ratified this declaration a few weeks later. The Communists remained interested in a new party, as shown by their continued agitation for a popular front. Perhaps of paramount importance was the fact that a large segment of the American public seemed to be attracted to the idea of third-party action. In an American Institute of Public Opinion poll, taken in December, 1936, 18 per cent of those questioned said that they would join a new farmer-labor party; by July, 1937, 21 per cent reported that they would join.[6]

The appeal of new-party action was strengthened by the development of several problems which harassed the Roosevelt administration in 1937 and early 1938. Dissension between labor leaders and the New Deal was quite apparent in 1937 because of the President's seeming impartiality in the bitter struggles between labor and industrial management, and the administration's tendency to ignore labor's advice on public policy.[7] Some labor leaders, particularly John L. Lewis of the United Mine Workers, openly discussed the possibility of a third party.[8] Sharp reductions in the number of recipients of public works employment and relief after the 1936 elections also disillusioned many political supporters of the New Deal. These economy measures placed a severe burden on state and local emergency-aid programs because industry could not absorb all those persons cut off from federal aid.[9] Vigorous protests against the reductions were made by a group of liberal governors that included Elmer A. Benson of Minnesota, Henry Horner of Illinois, Philip La Follette of Wisconsin, Herbert H. Lehman of New York, and Frank Murphy of Michigan. Another disillusioning factor was the strong Congressional opposition which confronted the President in 1937 and early 1938. The defeat of Roosevelt's proposals for executive and judicial reorganization, the emasculation of his slum-clearance plan, and the delays encountered in the passage of crop-control and wages-and-hours legislation, led many to conclude that he had lost control of Congress. Moreover, the administration's apparent inability to cope with the economic recession of 1937-1938 contributed significantly to liberal and radical dissatisfaction.[10] The ranks of the dissidents were further swelled when the President demanded increased naval and military expenditures. The sensitivity of many liberals and radicals to rearmament, especially its potential threat to civil liberties and economic stability, was heightened by Roosevelt's sudden interest in international collective security as revealed in his October, 1937, "Quarantine" speech.[11]

It was against the background of this apparent upsurge of dissatisfaction with the New Deal and the recent independent political successes that Philip F. La Follette of Wisconsin undertook to organize a national new-party movement—the National Progressives of America. Prior to 1938, Governor La Follette generally had supported the Roosevelt administration, although on occasion he vigorously quarreled with New Deal policies. While the party which he headed theoretically proclaimed its intention to expand into a national party in conjunction with independent liberal forces elsewhere, La Follette eschewed such action until 1938. He held that other independent state and local groups were, with few exceptions, too weak politically to establish a significant new national party. "Any sound political realignment must be built state by state," he said. "We learned in my father's campaign in 1924 that it can't be done overnight in the nation, but must be developed in the states after a great deal of organization work."[12] This conclusion was realistic in view

162

of President Roosevelt's attractiveness to most of the nation's liberals, and in view of the patronage and financial aid which the New Deal had extended to the Wisconsin Progressives. Soon after the 1936 elections, however, La Follette became convinced that the President had abandoned any idea of effecting permanent measures to solve the nation's basic economic problems. La Follette contended that the large-scale discharge of Works Progress Administration personnel in 1937 constituted the first proof of this abandonment. As Roosevelt was increasingly plagued by new domestic and foreign problems in 1937, La Follette concluded that not only was the President unable to deal with them, but, as a result, was losing the support of liberal leaders.[13] Another probable factor in La Follette's disaffection was the possible loss of political strength to the Democratic party. He feared that his party adherents, in voting for the Democrats nationally, might decide to desert the Wisconsin Progressive party altogether. In addition, the friendliness that had been manifest between Roosevelt and the Wisconsin third party had not been carried over into relations between the state's Democrats and Progressives. One Democratic party field agent, for example, protested to National Committee Chairman James A. Farley in 1936 that Wisconsin's Democratic leaders ignored the state's Republicans, but continually attacked the La Follette brothers, who were friendly to Roosevelt. The antagonism between the two parties was well illustrated by the successful move of Wisconsin's Democrats and

Republicans to wrest patronage control from the Progressives for the appointment of some 20,000 election officials.[14]

With these considerations in mind, Philip La Follette decided to work toward the formation of a new political movement in the United States. His own role in the movement, according to his conception of it, would be to help crystallize sentiment, to offer advice, and to interest independent liberal leaders in doing the detailed organizational work required to lay the basis for a new party. Starting in the spring of 1937, he began to lay the groundwork by corresponding and conferring with hundreds of possible new-party leaders.[15] La Follette's first public step toward forming a new movement was taken at the May, 1937, celebration commemorating the third anniversary of the founding of the Wisconsin Progressive party. At that time, he urged the country's liberals to co-operate with the Wisconsin Progressives in building a new major party. "The Progressive party has just begun to fight," he declared. "It looks forward to a national existence and to a national realignment. The time is close at hand for the formation of a new political realignment in the nation which will defeat the reactionary forces of the nation just as the Progressive party has defeated the reactionary forces of Wisconsin."[16] Later, Governor La Follette asserted in a speech in Des Moines that Roosevelt's "progressive leadership has been hamstrung by the swarm of reactionaries that infest the Democratic party."[17] Addressing a Labor Day celebration in Omaha, he lashed out at the "tweedledum and tweedledee politics [which] will destroy democracy in America," and asserted that a new political realignment must arise from "the vitality and liberalism of the middle west." Progress, he declared, would never result from a political party system in which liberals and conservatives were mixed helter-skelter in the two major parties; this could lead only to governmental inaction or some form of fascist dictatorship.[18]

In the summer of 1937, La Follette began to look for possible new party affiliates in other states. Through the efforts of Professor Paul H. Douglas, of the University of Chicago, he was put in touch with Raymond Haight, the leader of the California Progressive party. Haight, who had polled over 300,000 votes in the 1934 California gubernatorial election, was eager to expand the influence of his group through association with a national third party of liberals. After a good deal of investigation, La Follette concluded that the California Progressives would be welcome allies.[19] He also worked to gain the support of Mayor Fiorello La Guardia of New York, and to inspire the development and co-operation of the Iowa Farmer-Labor and Progressive movements. Meanwhile, La Follette continued to discuss economic ideas and new-party action during the fall and winter of 1937-1938 with grass roots farm, labor, white-collar, and small-business leaders.[20] With the exceptions of Douglas, Haight, and La Guardia, however, he avoided consulting recognized independent

165

and third-party leaders in regard to his political plans.

A clean break between Governor La Follette and the national administration came in April, 1938, when he vehemently attacked the New Deal's economic policies in a series of four radio talks. Referring to the existing recession, he declared that something was fundamentally wrong when after nine years of depression half of the American people were no better off than they had been in 1931. He recalled that after the election of 1936 the Progressives had urged upon the government the need for a sound, comprehensive, and carefully planned program. But "the national administration believed that the war on the depression had been won and that we were out of the woods," he declared. "Instead of a comprehensive program, it began to break camp, and to disband its army."[21] Condemning the policy of paying millions of people not to produce, La Follette called for a reorganization of the national economy to give the unemployed an opportunity to support themselves and thereby to add to the country's total wealth. He asserted that unified Progressive action was essential to make up for the failure of the New Deal.[22] Senator Robert La Follette meanwhile had been persuaded to join his brother in working for a new political movement. Late in 1937 and continuing into 1938, Senator La Follette had been sharply critical of the government's economic policies, and had indicated his basic disagreement with the administration's military program and foreign policies.

166

Typical of much of his criticism was his statement of April 24, 1938, in which he declared his opposition to Roosevelt's billion-dollar naval-expansion plan, and predicted that if the country geared its productive machinery to an expanding arms program, the worst depression in the world's history, and probably revolution, would occur when that expansion was stopped. He pleaded for a greater concentration on constructive internal improvements to replace the defeatist attitude "which says that we can do nothing but prepare for the inevitable war," and argued that a huge, low-cost housing program, for example, would be far more beneficial than building battleships and would provide more employment.[23]

These April speeches and statements by the La Follette brothers served as the immediate fanfare for the establishment of the National Progressives of America. Governor La Follette announced at the conclusion of his series of radio talks that a conference would be held in the University of Wisconsin Live Stock Pavilion on April 28, 1938, for the purpose of considering a reorganization of the liberal and progressive forces of the nation. Senator La Follette added that "a national third party is inevitable and now is the time to form one."[24] The Live Stock Pavilion meeting, compared with other Progressive conferences, was unusual in its trappings. The gathering was "protected" by national guardsmen in shiny steel helmets and was marked by the display of a red, white, and blue cross-and-circle emblem.[25] A capacity crowd of 3,500 people attended the meeting.

167

In an introductory speech, Judge Alvin Reis stressed that the liberal gains of the last five years would surely be lost if, as seemed probable, both the Democrats and the Republicans nominated conservative candidates for President in 1940. Progressives were urged by Judge Reis to prepare for such an event.[26] Governor La Follette gave the main address of the conference. He decried the world-wide retreat of democracy as evidenced by the "rise of dictators, the destruction of democracy and the spectre of another world war." "The failure to produce enough real wealth" had been at the base of this retreat because it had compelled people to support authoritarian-type governments to regulate the division of wealth. In the United States, he declared, the significance of these facts should be plain. The nation had to regain an economy of abundance in order to save traditional American liberties and to maintain and improve the standard of living.

In the course of his address La Follette dismissed, one by one, the current economic ideologies as instrumentalities incompetent to do the job. Economic plenty and security, he said, could not be derived from socialist share-the-wealth schemes or from the rugged individualism of classic capitalism. The first doctrine contradicted human nature in its impossible demand for absolute equality; the second was impractical in a society lacking a surplus of undeveloped natural resources. He also rejected Fascism and Communism as possible solutions to America's problems, because of their autocratic and coercive characteristics. In short, he insisted, the nation was not at a crossroad where it could turn to any one of these four ideologies. *"We are near the end of the road. The time has come when a new trail must be blazed—a trail that will take fundamental teachings of the past and apply them to the modern world as we know it. . . . We [must] have the right to try new ways, or to retain the old."* He called for modernization of the present form of government by giving the executive branch the power "to get things done." This could be accomplished, without threatening the people's liberties, by strengthening—as had been done in Wisconsin—the safeguards against abuse of power by government officials.

In discussing the actions which a reinvigorated American government should take to achieve national economic security, Governor La Follette cautioned that a perfected blueprint for action could not be devised in advance. The nation could aim in the "right direction," however, and learn from experimentation and practical experience how to deal with the details and contingencies. One of the first steps would be "to suppress . . . those stupid people who deny others access to materials that they themselves do not know rightly how to use." Then, the power of government would be used—regardless of cost—"to restore to every American the opportunity to help himself. After that he can sink or swim." This process, he said, would involve undertaking a series of projects which would not only give capital and

169

men the chance to work but would improve the nation's standard of living.

Using the nation's housing problem as an example, La Follette indicated the path which he thought could be followed in working on specific projects. He suggested that the procedures used in building streets and laying sewers might be adapted for improving the country's housing standards. First, an engineering and architectural plan would be drawn up, subject to the approval of the family affected. Second, the government would order that the plan be implemented. Third, easy financing arrangements would be made by the government between private capital and the family involved. Lastly, the construction work would be done, in so far as possible, by small contractors hired on the basis of a merit bid. The actual work should be done by private enterprise, he said, because "no government on earth can successfully manage, regulate and direct the numerous details that make for healthy families or successful business."

The address further contended that it was not difficult to think of or agree upon a series of national improvements which could put people back to work. The difficulty was in securing a government that had the resourcefulness and courage to act. The governor charged that the two old parties had proved their inability to accomplish the job. The Republican party, he held, was bankrupt in providing ideas and methods to enable democratic principles of economics and government to be maintained or to thrive. The Democrats, despite Roosevelt's "brilliant leadership," had been unable to cope with the tasks before the nation because of intraparty sabotaging and bickering. "When there are basic issues to be met, leadership alone, no matter how great, can not mix political oil and water."

Governor La Follette then announced the formation of the National Progressives of America, the organization which he claimed could solve the nation's economic problems in an effective yet democratic fashion. "This is no 'popular front,' no conglomeration of conflicting, opposing forces huddled together for temporary expediency." The new movement would seek "only those who come with complete conviction, and without reservation. The movement that unites America, must be itself united. . . . Definitely and irrevocably we are in the lists to stay until the American people recapture their heritage. Make no mistake, this is NOT a *third* party. As certain as the sun rises, we are launching THE party of our time."[27]

The establishment of the new organization immediately caught the attention of the press; the National Progressives of America was front-page news throughout the country. This publicity was probably responsible for the sizable amount of public and political reaction to the movement. Within a month after its organization was announced, Governor La Follette's office received some 25,000 letters concerning the proposed party, most of them praising it. The American Institute of Public Opinion con-

171

ducted a survey in May and found that 64 per cent of those interviewed had heard of the National Progressives of America. One out of every nine of those who were familiar with the movement indicated interest in joining it.[28]

The reaction of liberal and radical leaders to the National Progressives was generally not encouraging. Senator George W. Norris, the elder statesman of progressivism, voiced the fears of many liberals when he stated that the new organization might split liberal forces.[29] Herbert Hoover gave support to Norris' concern when he expressed the hope that the National Progressives might serve as a divisive element in the New Deal coalition and thereby aid the Republicans to return to power.[30] Typical of the response of agricultural leaders was the comment of K. W. Hones, the head of the Wisconsin branch of the National Farmers' Union: "I don't believe the rank and file of farmers are going to give up what they have, no matter how little it is, unless they are cocksure of something better." Hones indicated that his apathy was prompted partly by the fact that "we and Labor have not been asked to sit in on the inside to discuss it."[31] The labor press and major labor leaders, in the main, avoided comment, although the letters Governor La Follette received from minor trade union officials usually revealed sympathy with the organization's aims. The general silence of major labor leaders and organs might be explained largely by two factors. First, they were concentrating much of their time and resources on the battle between the

American Federation of Labor and the new Congress of Industrial Organizations. Second, in view of President Roosevelt's renewed campaign to secure legislation favorable to labor, especially the Fair Labor Standards bill, they were in no position to break with the New Deal leaders. Had the President failed to gain passage of the measures desired by organized labor, many labor leaders would conceivably have shown interest in new-party action later in the year. This was illustrated by the threat of David Dubinsky of the International Ladies' Garment Workers to declare in favor of a new party if the Democrats repudiated the New Deal program.[32]

The major magazines of liberal persuasion differed in their estimates of the National Progressives. The *New Republic* believed that Governor La Follette's criticisms had much merit, but added that "it is obviously too early to say whether a third party will be either desirable or necessary in the 1940 election." The magazine saw the organization as a weapon which would operate to exert pressure on the Democratic party for more liberal action.[33] *Common Sense* called upon liberals to try to reinvigorate the New Deal. It hoped that the National Progressives would not interfere with this attempt, but rather would stand as a reserve organization for liberals should the New Deal collapse.[34] *Christian Century* analyzed the La Follette maneuver as serving "notice on Mr. Roosevelt that if his party adopts a conservative or equivocal course in 1940 it must prepare to suffer the loss of vitally important liberal votes." The periodical lauded the National Progressives' objectives as constituting "a liberal program which is neither Marxist nor fascist in its origins, but which gives promise of attacking the roots of our economic problem as the New Deal has never done."[35] On the other hand, the *Nation* was disturbed because it could find "no indication of a genuine farmer-labor base for [La Follette's] program." This magazine branded the National Progressives "middle class," and declared that it would regard the new organization with "critical sympathy."[36]

Caution or outright rejection characterized the reaction of other third-party groups. Spokesmen for the American Labor party were skeptical of the program. Moreover, they saw no necessity for a new national party so long as President Roosevelt fought for liberal legislation.[37] The Minnesota Farmer-Laborites announced that although they would continue to support President Roosevelt's program, they would watch the development of the National Progressives with "sympathy and friendship." The Minnesota group appointed a committee of five to study the organization.[38] Norman Thomas, the 1936 Socialist candidate for President, hailed La Follette's analysis of the defects of the New Deal, and remarked that his party would view the movement sympathetically.[39] The Socialist party executive committee, however, later charged that the new organization represented a move toward fascism. The committee labeled the new party's program "a shocking disappointment," which "offers the workers and farmers no more than the Republicans, [and] less than the New Deal."[40] The Communist response was understandably vigorous. Calling the National Progressives' objectives "reactionary" and "phony," the Communist party declared that the new group would split America's progressives.[41] Mayor La Guardia, in commenting on La Follette's proposals, indicated that there was not so much need for a new party as for progressive unity.[42] The only enthusiastic response to the formation of the National Progressives from a third-party leader came from Representative William Lemke, the Union party's 1936 presidential candidate.[43]

President Roosevelt showed no public concern over Governor La Follette's new venture. Privately, however, the President revealed interest in the development of the movement. He was well aware that the National Progressives could injure state and national Democratic election efforts in 1938 and 1940 by siphoning off liberal votes.[44] Moreover, he told Secretary of the Interior Harold Ickes that unless La Follette went too far, the National Progressives would demonstrate to Democratic leaders that they were in danger of losing the liberal support necessary to victory in 1940.[45] Commenting further on the organization in a personal letter to Ambassador William Phillips, the President wrote:

Did you know that Phil La Follette started his Third Party with a huge meeting in Wisconsin, the chief feature of which was the dedication of a new emblem—a twenty foot wide banner with a red circle and a blue cross on it?

175

While the crowd present was carried away with the enthusiasm of the moment, most of the country seem to think that this was a feeble imitation of the Swastika. All that remains is for some major party to adopt a new form of arm salute. I have suggested the raising of both arms above the head, followed by a bow from the waist. At least this will be good for people's figures![46]

Despite the discouraging initial response of independent political groups to the National Progressives, its leaders set out to build the movement into a strong national political force. Many challenging problems confronted them. Funds had to be raised, a headquarters established, lieutenants recruited and disciplined, literature written, mailing lists compiled, correspondence answered, hostile election laws complied with, and, of greatest importance, voters attracted. The work of attacking these problems began immediately after the formation of the National Progressive group. Governor La Follette began the campaign by making a series of speeches in Iowa, including one in Des Moines which was broadcast over a national radio network. In an address in Cedar Rapids he declared that the party hoped to have Congressional candidates in ten states by fall. He urged the people of Iowa to support the formation of a united Progressive party in that state, but pointed out that such an organization could come only from the people and not from leaders.[47] Throughout the summer and fall of 1938, the Wisconsin governor continued to speak on behalf of the National Progressives in the Middle West and the

East. Senator Robert La Follette in his speeches and radio addresses also gave support to the new organization, as did General Ralph Immel, its executive director. An office was established in Madison to handle mail and the raising of funds. The Progressive party of California, running Raymond Haight for governor, became the affiliate in that state. In Iowa, a Farmer-Labor ticket, representing the National Progressive forces there, was entered in the 1938 election contests. By September, groups in Idaho, North Dakota, and Oregon were connected with the La Follette organization, and factions of liberals in Illinois and Texas were negotiating for the establishment of connections.[48]

Early in the fall, however, it was apparent that the new party was not meeting with signal success. Raymond Haight received only about 254,000 votes out of over two million cast in California's August primaries, and this did not augur victory in that state.[49] In Iowa, there was little popular enthusiasm for the National Progressives. The other state groups declared that they were not yet ready to enter the electoral lists.[50] These difficulties seemed to indicate that the party's potential appeal to liberals had been greatly reduced by the endeavors of the national administration to offset the liberal dissatisfaction which had developed in 1937 and early 1938. The enactment in 1938 of the second Agricultural Adjustment Act and of legislation regulating wages and hours, combined with a spectacular upsurge in federal public works employment and the New Deal's trust-busting program, worked to restore liberal confidence in President Roosevelt. The President endeared himself to many other liberals by his intensive, although unsuccessful, efforts to purge the Democratic party of conservative officeholders.

Meanwhile, Governor La Follette seemed to be losing political strength in Wisconsin. Although most of the state's Progressives gave either tacit or enthusiastic support to his organization, an important minority refused to endorse it. The widely read Madison *Capital Times,* the semiofficial newspaper of the Wisconsin Progressive party, announced that "if repudiation of Pres. Roosevelt is to be a requisite of joining this new venture, the *Capital Times* is frank in saying that it will not go along."[51] The newspaper also called the National Progressive program vague, and even suggested that the methods used in staging the Live Stock Pavilion meeting were comparable to Nazi and Fascist techniques.[52] The powerful Farmer-Labor Progressive Federation, which included the organized farm, labor, and socialist supporters of the Wisconsin Progressive party, adopted a "hands off" policy toward the new organization.[53] Eleven prominent Progressives, including Paul R. Alfonsi, the speaker of the lower house of the state legislature, charged that the National Progressives tended "to split the unity of the people." This group noted with alarm that the new party, "While making no attack on Wall Street monopolies, makes sharp attacks on the standards of organized labor and on relief and the W. P. A."[54]

Other problems embarrassed the Progressives at home. William T. Evjue, the editor of the *Capital Times*, laid the foundation for effective Republican and Democratic attacks against his own party by his forthright criticisms of the conduct of party and governmental affairs in Wisconsin. Evjue's disagreement with Progressive leaders stemmed from Governor La Follette's attempts to secure passage of his 1937 legislative proposals. When the regular session of the legislature adjourned without enacting the governor's program for social and economic welfare, he called a special session to meet in September, 1937. Again the members procrastinated in considering the proposed legislation, and a week before the scheduled adjournment date, he demanded that action be taken on the controversial measures. Legislative leaders, therefore, with the governor's encouragement, abandoned some of the customary parliamentary procedures. Evjue unrestrainedly characterized this portion of the session as "a week in which we had legislation by executive decree," and charged La Follette and his capitol supporters with using "tactics of Huey Long variety." Although the editor declared that he favored the measures enacted, he warned that "two can play this game," and that the incident afforded reactionaries an undesirable precedent.[55] From this time on, Evjue's editorials continued to be extremely critical of the expediency and personal ambition which he felt increasingly marked Progressive government and politics in Wisconsin.[56]

179

Many other incidents occurred which not only allowed the opposition parties to make political capital but created unrest within the Wisconsin Progressive party. Important among these were the summary dismissal of the popular president of the University of Wisconsin, Dr. Glenn Frank; the conviction of one of La Follette's aides of manslaughter in connection with an automobile mishap; charges of political coercion of Works Progress Administration employees by the Progressive party; accusations of illegal use of old-age beneficiary lists for political purposes; and the doubtful Wisconsin residency of the 1938 Progressive candidate for United States senator. The virtual snubbing of the Progressive Youth League and the Farmer-Labor Progressive Federation in determining party policies antagonized those groups, and the Federation tried to defeat the governor for renomination in the 1938 primary election. While its candidate was beaten by a four-to-one margin, the Federation's activities revealed an amount of dissatisfaction that had not been apparent in previous Progressive gubernatorial primaries. Governor La Follette's inadequacy in dealing with these situations resulted largely from the difficulty involved in trying to serve effectively both as governor and as head of a national political organization. Not only was the administration of government and party affairs in Wisconsin consequently impaired, but his efforts on behalf of the National Progressives of America also suffered.

180

The misfortunes and mistakes of the governor and the Wisconsin Progressives in 1937 and 1938 heartened the state's Democrats and Republicans. Powerful factions in these two parties ran gubernatorial candidates in the 1938 primary elections on coalition or "Stop La Follette" platforms. They agreed that the old-party nominee who received the least number of primary votes would withdraw in favor of the other. In compliance with this bargain, the Democratic gubernatorial nominee renounced his candidacy and endorsed Republican Julius P. Heil.[57] This maneuver, combined with exploitation of the many charges against the state administration and disgruntlement within Progressive ranks, led to Governor La Follette's defeat in the November election. Heil received 543,675 votes to 353,381 cast for the incumbent. La Follette's decisive rejection at the hands of the Wisconsin voters was accompanied by an equally clear repudiation of the state's Progressive party. The party lost control of the other four statewide elective offices and retained only two of its seven seats in the national House of Representatives. The Progressive delegation in the state legislature dropped from forty-nine to thirty-two in the assembly, and from eighteen to eleven in the senate.[58]

The fate of the National Progressive affiliates in Iowa and California in 1938 was even more dismal. In California, the Progressive program for economic reconstruction failed to divert public attention from the battle waged between Republican and Democratic forces over old-age benefits. Progressive guber-

181

natorial candidate Raymond Haight polled only 64,-
418 ballots out of over 2,600,000 cast in the California election.[59] In Iowa, the National Progressive
candidates failed to obtain the 2 per cent minimum
of the total vote which was necessary to qualify their
party for a permanent place on the ballot.[60]

Although faced with these severe defeats, Governor La Follette declared his intention of going on
with the National Progressives of America. He saw
the reverses that liberals in general suffered in the
1938 elections as proving "more than ever the vital
necessity for a new national movement. Both the old
parties are firmly in the control of reactionaries. A
few years practical demonstration will again show
the incapacity of reactionaries to meet the problems
of our day. . . . The National Progressives of America
goes forward today. Around it, liberals and progressives throughout the nation will rally."[61] Despite
these optimistic words, the party was maintained
only as a paper organization, held in reserve for independent liberal action in the event that both major
parties should nominate conservative presidential
candidates in 1940. With the nomination of Roosevelt for a third term, however, the movement was
completely abandoned.

In form, if not in goals, the National Progressives
of America seemed to represent something new on
the American scene. It was an attempt by some progressives to unite for constructive political action the
nation's liberals and moderate conservatives, those
who thought that private enterprise merited a future

in American society, but who believed in more government action to control it. In this respect, therefore, it was conceived as a means of perpetuating the power of independent liberal politicians. That the movement failed was due only incidentally to the political mismanagement from which it occasionally suffered. Basically important was the fact that liberals and progressives could achieve some of their goals by co-operating with the Democratic party. As long as this was true, most of them would be unwilling to commit themselves irrevocably to any new-party attempt. Of special significance was the fact—as witnessed in the 1938 and 1940 elections—that the public was growing apathetic to attempts at reform. Ironically, even liberal, progressive, and radical leaders were becoming less concerned with domestic matters as international tensions developed. These factors not only contributed to the failure of the National Progressives, but undercut serious support for left-of-center action in general after the middle of 1938. Thenceforth, radicals, progressives, and even liberals were to find it imperative to revise drastically their economic and social thinking. Even though most of them responded to this requirement, they were to discover that the ideas of establishing a potent new party or capturing an old party were chimerical in the World War II and Cold War eras. The best they could hope for was to maintain a small portion of their former influence and vigor by working within the Democratic and Republican parties.

Chapter VII
LOOKING BACKWARD

The activities of the independent liberal, progressive, and radical movements of the 1930's were based upon motivating factors which were basic to organizational success. Demands for economic, political, and social changes were multitudinous, and the dissident groups were not lacking in able, ambitious leaders and thinkers. Yet the American leftwing was unable to capitalize on these assets so as to become a formidable competitor for control of the organs of government. That the left-of-center movements failed in this respect was attributable to their inability to overcome four general sets of obstacles: internal weaknesses, social-psychological attitudes of potential followers, the political strategy of the Democratic party, and practical problems of organization.

One of the most obvious features of American politics has been the schisms that have consistently rent any attempt to oppose the dominant political parties. The movements of the 1930's offer an excellent series of illustrations of this characteristic in that they seemed to be disunited in every possible way. The most manifest division concerned differences of opinion as to the kind of vehicle which should be used in attaining political success. There were those who, like George Norris, generally rejected the idea of party, holding that only independent voting would lead to true democracy. Men like Upton Sinclair argued that infiltration of the Democratic party constituted the best method of gaining political power. A few people, mainly in agricultural and labor ranks, felt that only pressure-group action would work. Most left-of-center leaders, however, often thought of third-party action. In this area, there were four discernible idealistic groupings: first, those Marxists who called either for expansion of pre-depression third parties or the creation of new, tightly organized revolutionary parties; second, those who worked for the formation of a new, farmer-labor-intellectual party, with the hope that it would replace one of the major parties and receive a popular mandate to reorganize the federal government; third, those liberal Republicans and conservative Socialists who felt that the local Democratic, Republican, and Socialist organizations were impossible vehicles for change, but concluded that Roosevelt as an individual was a true heir of progressivism (the latter were more interested in supporting the President with independent local organizations than they were in establishing a new national party); fourth, those who stood with one foot in the new-party camp and the other in that of the Democratic party and whose strategy—for example, that of Labor's Non-Partisan League—was to threaten new-party action in order to gain concessions from the Democratic party.

Another internal weakness was that while the left-of-center movements agreed that American society was in a bad state, they were unable to concur

185

on how things ought to be. Only on their immediate economic demands did they achieve any degree of uniformity. They were practically unanimous on issues such as low-interest government refinancing of farm and home debts, the rights of farm and labor organizations, and the taxation of securities. In attempting to plan a long-range economic program, however, they were unable to formulate an equation which could satisfy at the same time the interests of farm, labor, intellectual, and small-business dissidents. The left-of-center movements could not overcome their doctrinal rigidities or transcend their emotionally charged slogans. Therefore, innumerable plans were presented for the nationalization of resources and enterprises. Multifarious systems of producers' and consumers' co-operatives were suggested; a hundred different programs for a mixed economy were submitted. These various plans for a reconstituted economic system were always accompanied by demands for a more efficient government controlled by an alert, democratically oriented citizenry. Here again the proposed paths to salvation were confusing. Offering such measures as recall, proportional representation, and referendum, they were quite aware that these would be effective weapons against tyranny only if citizens were prepared to participate actively and intelligently in politics. It was contended, ironically enough, that "enlightened self-interest," which was derided in the economic sphere, would work to increase democracy. One other area of the proposals made by the political independents illustrated their disunity on what ought to be done. Vociferously opposing the use of war as a national policy, they were divided on how permanent peace for this nation or the world might be achieved. For example, some said that a universal strike of workers and farmers would stop any threat of war, while others preached the doctrine of collective security. Isolationists insisted that their way was the most practical. There were even some political independents who declared for the creation of a strong international agency to solve the world's problems peacefully. The end goals of the liberals and radicals were laudable, yet in proposing methods to achieve a just economy, a democratic polity, and permanent peace, they resembled those who are against sin. They were unable to agree on a plausible program long enough to consider adequately the strategic problems involved in gaining control of the agencies of change.

A final important weakness within the ranks of the advocates of change was their failure to show a reasonably united front on the matter of leadership. Would Nye accept Sinclair as the leader? would the La Follettes accept Olson as the leader? would Dewey accept Lemke? would Thomas accept any of them? and so on. One statement by George Norris illustrated this situation quite nicely: "When Phil La Follette was governor of Wisconsin, I sought to persuade him to undertake the unicameral reform there. The chief difficulty in all undertakings of this kind is that the outstanding [liberal] political leaders do not take kindly to a movement of this nature unless it originates with them. So often they seem to be jealous if it develops outside their own domain."[1] As was observed of the March, 1935, conference of progressive Congressmen, independents were too often unable to subordinate their favorite personal projects to work wholeheartedly for more important measures sponsored by their confreres. In Congress they might vote together, but when it came to trying to obtain citizen or legislative support for progressive proposals it was each man for himself. To be sure, this inability to develop over-all leadership was in part motivated by the sincere skepticism of some leaders as to the superiority of their colleagues, but just as important a consideration was the obstructionism of others who placed their personal ambitions foremost. In any event, it seemed that progressives were so accustomed to the habit of independence that when it came to making a concerted effort politically or legislatively they could not work together as a team.

The second area of obstacles that the left-of-center movements of the 1930's had to surmount was the attitudes of many of their potential followers regarding American society and their place in it. First of all, as Rudolf Heberle has pointed out, most people will not participate in political movements unless stimulated by some extraordinary situation.[2] In the United States, several factors countered the special event of the depression, which seemingly should have roused close to total political participation. Many citizens, even those adversely affected by the depression, had no conception of the causes of it. Some thought it to be a personal problem that could be solved only in a personal manner; others were willing to grab at and to hold on to the first straw of relief offered to them.[3] Then, too, as Hadley Cantril stated, institutionalized programs frequently appeared "to the single individual as comparatively impersonal or remote. It is not easy for a busy, worried, uneducated person, already harassed with pressing problems of his own that demand immediate solution, to see the significance in his life of a certain foreign policy, a certain agricultural subsidy, or a certain regulation of the stock exchange."[4] Moreover, there was a discernible contrast in the progressive-radical leaders' outlook and that of much of their potential following. The critical ability of the former had been created by broad or meaningful education and experience which led to their acceptance of complex, not commonly accepted values. The latter, who were usually restricted in education and experience, identified themselves to such an extent with the psychological and material objects surrounding them that only a constant barrage of propaganda could hope to change their viewpoints.[5] These restricting factors of pressing needs and narrow experience were augmented by a partly resultant basic lack of class consciousness in American society. Partly owing to the traditionally well-publicized possibilities of socio-economic improvement and to community disapproval of political "eccentricity," groups proposing

189

working-class solidarity found it difficult, with their limited resources, to convince a large number of people to vote for anything—be it right or wrong—that was far removed from "middle-class" concepts.[6] Then, too, it is not implausible that the lifelong political habits of those voters who sought social explanations for the depression were controlling factors in determining their readiness to find relief only in the two old parties. It was only with great effort that so many voters were able to switch from one major party to the other; it was even more difficult to prepare them to participate in a new political organism, especially when it was tinged with utopianism and often expressed itself in emotionally discomforting language. For example, it was not necessarily political sagacity that caused North Dakotans in 1936 to reject William Lemke as a candidate for President while returning him to Congress as a Republican.

Another social-psychological barrier seemed to be that a large number of Americans have an instinctive desire to be on the winning side. Such a desire, if it exists in relation to politics, could be a great hindrance to progressive and radical movements in obtaining power. But just as unfortunate was the wish of those who were willing to take a chance on a possible loser but who wanted to make their cause a winner at once. The building of a successful new movement with a radical or a progressive program was not to be achieved overnight, and such an organization was unable to accommodate the "hurry" complex of its followers. Many of the left-of-center leaders in the 1930's were aware of some of these psychological problems. Paul Douglas cited "the reluctance which most Americans feel towards associating themselves with lonely causes and small movements . . . their preference for immersion in the crowd, and . . . their great joy in riding band wagons, irrespective of their destiny." He asserted that, in combating the "natural tendency for the American mind to work through existing political agencies in preference to creating new ones," "it will not be enough to raise the banner." The advocates of change knew that it would be necessary "to build an organization in virtually every township, ward and precinct, which will stick to its job through the years."[7] The question, never satisfactorily answered, was, how was this to be done?

The independent political movements encountered a third barrier to success in Franklin D. Roosevelt and the Democratic party. It must be stressed that historically the nation's major parties have been sufficiently responsive to demands for change to prevent a large number of voters from shifting their loyalties to a third political force. Of course, this responsiveness has usually been spurred by the part independent political groups play in giving expression to discontent. As soon as the solutions to critical problems that are proposed by independent movements have gained some popular approval, such suggested remedies are usually given serious consideration by the major parties. When the major parties adopt dissident proposals as a part of their own pro-

191

grams, dissenting groups discover not only that they aided the objects of their contempt but that they have inadvertently stripped themselves of their appeal to the electorate.[8] Democratic leaders were not long in assuming their roles in this traditional game of American politics. Although many progressives and radicals felt that the concessions granted were designed mainly to appease them and the discontented of the land rather than to effect fundamental remedies, such concessions seemed sufficient to maintain the Democratic party's power. Most of the discontented feared, not necessarily without reason, that by risking independent political action, they might lose what they had gained under the New Deal, regardless of how little it was.

The New Deal was also able to frustrate the organizational ambitions of political independents in a more deliberate and concrete fashion. As has been seen, federal patronage and spoils were put at the disposal of groups like the Wisconsin Progressives and the Minnesota Farmer-Laborites. Moreover, independent-minded liberals and radicals were given opportunities to advance to positions of importance in the Democratic party and in the government. In these ways, the Roosevelt administration was able to weaken dissident groups quite effectively. Samuel Lubbell has cited an excellent illustration of the results of such maneuvers:

The sirens screeched through the night as the limousine sped along the New Jersey highway to Passaic where a 1936 Roosevelt campaign rally was being held. It was the first

192

time in his life that David Dubinsky had ever had a police
escort. Never the quiet meditative type, Dubinsky was
bug-eyed with excitement. Turning to two union aides, he
began reminiscing of the days when he first became interested in politics.

Meyer London was running for Congress on the Socialist ticket in New York City, and recalled Dubinsky, "I made
speeches from a soapbox and was an election watcher. I
slept for three nights with my wrist strapped to the ballot
box so Tammany leaders wouldn't throw the box into the
river. Now look at me! In a limousine! With a police escort!"

Sinking back into the luxuriously plushed seat, Dubinsky
sighed, "I wonder whether I would do all that over
again?"[9]

The administration's stratagems, Roosevelt's appealing political personality, and the fact that "the New
Deal gave evidence that you could do progressive
things with an old party,"[10] combined to form a
most important obstacle to the political unity of
progressives and radicals in the 1930's.

The fourth set of barriers to independent political action could be described as practical ones. If
a group aimed at building a third party, it was
hampered by vexing state regulations for obtaining
and keeping ballot privileges. In Illinois, a new party
was required to present a petition containing 25,000
signatures, with at least 200 coming from each of 50
of the state's counties; Arkansas demanded a fee of
$327.50 for filing each petition of candidacy; many
states commanded that each of the petition signatures
be notarized, a process which cost money and took
time.[11] Furthermore, the single-member district sys-

tem of election meant that a third party would have a difficult time in gaining voting majorities in enough election districts to be effective in the various legislative bodies. This problem was even further complicated by the plethora of economic- and social-interest groups that had to be canvassed. The job of campaigning in thousands of legislative constituencies and interest groups seemed a forbidding task in itself. In addition, lack of funds always plagued left-of-center movements. Their supporters often received letters similar to this one sent by the American Commonwealth Political Federation: "We are hard hit financially. Our national organizer has been months behind in salary and often we have to ask the office staff to wait a few days for their checks."[12] Money was needed for publicity to circumvent an often hostile or indifferent press; money was needed for organizers who could train the green recruits of the organization into something resembling an adroit political force; money was needed to meet the costs of research, clerical aid, travel, and communication. It was discouraging to realize that a political group which appealed to the economically lower classes could not count on gaining adequate funds from that source. True at any time, this fact was aggravated by the effects of the depression. These practical problems could never be dismissed as minor, for the only way to solve them was by persuading the voters of the truth of left-of-center viewpoints. This required large-scale organization and publicity campaigns that obviously demanded larger

194

amounts of money than those which the political independents could command. In view of the obstacles to new-party activity in the 1930's, the wonder was not that these groups failed to secure dominant power, but rather that they gained as much influence as they did.

In analyzing the left-of-center independents of the 1930's, one must emphasize that their failures were mainly in terms of political organization. They did, in other areas, achieve some success. They contributed much to educating the voters, the government, and the major parties in the bases of dissidence and in possible answers to the questions raised by the discontented. Though it is difficult to trace precisely the links between left-wing activities and government programs, one may assert that the dissidents not only helped to maintain the pressures which gave impetus to New Deal liberalism but often planted the seeds of national policy. Dissident leaders vigorously pointed out what they considered to be the main defects in American society and eagerly recommended solutions to those problems. There were many effective way in which this was done. The independent liberals, progressives, and radicals who held office introduced and debated legislation, influenced bureaucrats, and persisted in trying to convert their more conservative fellow-officeholders. Politically independent leaders devoted a great deal of time to using public meetings, newspapers, magazines, and radio facilities to air their opinions. The journals for which they usually wrote—*Common*

Sense, the *New Republic,* the *Nation,* and the *Christian Century*—were widely read in Washington, especially in the executive offices. Moreover, the *New York Times,* which afforded political independents remarkably good news coverage, was certain to be read carefully in the capital during the Roosevelt years. Furthermore, the progressives and radicals pressed their ideas upon the government as well as the electorate by utilizing the organizations which they were able to develop. By contesting or threatening to contest the Presidency and state and Congressional posts in elections, they kept the political situation fluid. The organizational victories in Minnesota and Wisconsin of independents and the development of serious political threats on the West Coast resulted in appeasement of the progressives by the national administration. The well-publicized flirtations between the political independents and agrarian and labor leaders stimulated the Democratic party to take action on agricultural and industrial problems. By co-operating politically with the New Deal when they did, many progressives and liberals put the President and some of his lieutenants under obligations to them. This enabled left-of-center politicians to secure administration support for some of their domestic proposals, and also allowed them to contribute to the maintenance of a passive American foreign policy from 1933 to 1937.[13] That the Democratic party gave political independents opportunities for power and prestige served to indicate that the thought and activities of these movements had considerable influence in the 1930's.

This influence did not come without a price. Through their contributions to the New Deal's success in legislating and administering reforms, independent liberals, progressives, and radicals aided in siphoning off pressure for more far-reaching accomplishments. Moreover, by accepting aid from the national administration, many left-wingers formed a habit of dependence which they were eventually unwilling to do without. One may conjecture that as a result of these "successes"—as well as of their failures—by 1939 progressivism and radicalism were removed as important conceptual and organizational forces in American life. The political conditions of the eras of the second World War and the Cold War apparently made it impossible for them to return to positions of prominence. In fact, even the liberalism of the 1950's—a liberalism which generally gained the support of progressive and radical remnants—only faintly resembled the left-of-center politics of the 1930's. It is perhaps ironic that, in the 1950's, liberalism's heroes had become Dean Acheson, Alben Barkley, Adlai Stevenson, and Harry Truman, men who would not have been well regarded by left-of-center forces twenty years earlier. But situations change, and so do men. Some men forget; others learn.

197

NOTES

I

1. *Nation*, Dec. 26, 1928, p. 702.
2. *New York Times*, Sept. 9, 1929, p. 1.
3. League for Independent Political Action, *Wanted: A New Political Alignment* (New York, 1930), p. 1. It should be noted that many Socialists were interested in the League, as shown by the membership of such Socialist leaders as Maurer, Laidler, and Blanshard. If political realignment was to occur, the Socialists wanted a voice in the new political order.
4. League for Independent Political Action, *Wanted*, pp. 2 f.; Paul H. Douglas, *The Coming of a New Party* (New York, 1932), pp. 180 ff.
5. League for Independent Political Action, *Wanted*, pp. 2 f.
6. LIPA counted on psychological motivations, to some extent, to gain a mass following for a new party. "There are at least two sources of emotional reinforcement which one may tap and which should give courage to go on. The first is the fascination of the process, while the second is the importance of the objects sought. . . . There will come also the satisfaction of serving a worthy cause which is far greater than oneself. . . . And if ultimate failure is, nevertheless, the result, there will still be the joy of going down under a worthy flag." Douglas (see note 4), pp. 223 f.
7. League for Independent Political Action, *Wanted*, pp. 3 f.
8. *Ibid.*, pp. 5 f.
9. Howard Y. Williams, "Do Americans Want a New Party," *World Tomorrow*, July, 1930, pp. 294 ff.
10. *New York Times*, Dec. 26, 1930, pp. 1 ff.
11. *Ibid.*, pp. 1 f.
12. Richard L. Neuberger and Stephen B. Kahn, *Integrity—the Life of George W. Norris* (New York, 1937), pp. 184 ff.
13. *New York Times*, Dec. 31, 1930, p. 3.
14. Douglas, p. 172.
15. *New York Times*, Dec. 30, 1930, p. 3.
16. *Proceedings of a Conference of Progressives, March 11 and 12, 1931* (Washington, 1931), pp. 3 and 7.
17. *New Republic*, Jan. 7, 1931, pp. 203 ff.; March 18, pp. 111 ff.
18. Howard Y. Williams, LIPA's chief organizer, was a Minnesotan, and devoted a good deal of time to trying to gain the unrestricted support of the Minnesota Farmer-Labor party for the League's goals. He was aided by the sympathy of men like William Mahoney, one of the Minnesota party's founders, and Henry G. Teigan, editor of the official organ of the party, the *Farmer-Labor Leader*.
19. *Farmer-Labor Leader*, Jan. 28, 1932, p. 3.
20. *Ibid.*
21. The National Farmer-Labor party is not to be confused with the Minnesota Farmer-Labor party. There were neither official connections nor friendly feelings between the two organizations.
22. *New York Times*, April 28, 1932, p. 2; May 5, p. 2; May 7, p. 3; June 18, p. 1; June 26, p. 21; and July 11, p. 3.
23. *Washington Star*, Jan. 7, 1932, p. 1; *The Progressive* (Madison), Jan. 16, 1932, p. 1; and *New York Times*, Jan. 17, 1932, p. 1.

24. *New York Times,* April 3, 1932, p. 24; April 3, sec. III, p. 5; April 18, p. 17.
25. *Ibid.,* July 17, 1932, p. 2.
26. *Ibid.,* July 5, 1932, p. 4; July 9, p. 3; Aug. 18, p. 3.
27. *Ibid.,* Aug. 15, 1932, pp. 2 f.; Aug. 17, p. 2; Aug. 18, p. 3.
28. *Ibid.,* Sept. 22, 1932, p. 17; Oct. 13, p. 3.
29. *Ibid.,* Oct. 10, 1931, p. 2.
30. Douglas, pp. 169 ff.
31. *New York Times,* Feb. 1, 1932, p. 7.
32. *Ibid.,* March 8, 1932, p. 3.
33. The Socialists were never remiss in reminding the apostles of new farmer-labor party action that they had lost their place on the ballot in seventeen states after the "marriage" of 1924; Robert Morss Lovett, "A Party in Embryo," *New Republic,* July 24, 1935, pp. 295-297. For an interesting discussion regarding this problem see Scott D. Johnson, "The Socialists and La Follette Progressivism," *Institute of Social Studies Bulletin* (Rand School), winter, 1952, pp. 87, 94.
34. *Farmer-Labor Leader,* June 25, 1931, p. 1.
35. George H. Mayer, *The Political Career of Floyd B. Olson* (Minneapolis, 1951), pp. 96 ff; *New York Times,* April 10, 1932, sec. III, p. 5.
36. A brief discussion of progressive efforts in support of Roosevelt's 1932 campaign is included in Donald R. McCoy, "The Progressive National Committee of 1936," *Western Political Quarterly,* June, 1956, pp. 455 f.
37. Henry G. Teigan MSS, Devere Allen to Teigan, June 22, 1932.
38. Emmanuel Davidove, LIPA chairman, Cleveland, Ohio, in the *Cleveland Plain Dealer,* July 8, 1932, p. 7.
39. Statement by Howard Y. Williams, personal interview, April 23, 1952.
40. *Nation,* Feb. 17, 1932, sec. II (full text); see the *Cleveland Plain Dealer,* July 9, 1932, pp. 1 ff., for conference revisions.
41. *New York Times,* July 10, 1932, p. 12; *Cleveland Plain Dealer,* July 10, 1932, p. 1.
42. *Cleveland Plain Dealer,* July 11, 1932, p. 1. See the following articles for sympathetic and "semi-official" accounts of the League's Cleveland Conference: Robert Morss Lovett, "Progressives at Cleveland," *New Republic,* July 20, 1932, pp. 258 f.; Devere Allen, "A Progressive for Revolt," *Nation,* July 27, 1932, pp. 80 ff.; and John Dewey, "Prospects for a Third Party," *New Republic,* July 27, 1932, pp. 278 ff.
43. *Cleveland Plain Dealer,* July 10, 1932, p. 6.
44. *New York Times,* July 24, 1932, sec. II, p. 1.
45. *New Republic,* July 20, 1932, p. 245.
46. *Christian Century,* July 20, 1932, p. 917.
47. Illustrative of this was the "Open Letter to the People of the United States," signed by John Dewey and 500 economists, which was circulated for the benefit of the nation's press. This document was mainly concerned with discussing LIPA policies and goals; the endorsement of Norman Thomas was mentioned almost incidentally.
48. Howard Y. Williams, "Mr. Thomas and the LIPA," *Nation,* Feb. 1, 1933; David A. Shannon, *The Socialist Party of America* (New York, 1955), p. 222.
49. *News Bulletin of the League for Independent Political Action,* November-December, 1932, p. 1.

50. *Ibid.*, p. 2.
51. *New York Times,* July 18, 1932, p. 30; Sept. 17, p. 17; Sept. 9, p. 4.
52. *Ibid.,* March 12, 1932, p. 3; May 14, p. 14.
53. Theodore Saloutos and John D. Hicks, *Agricultural Discontent in the Middle West, 1900-1939* (Madison, 1951), pp. 443 ff.

II

1. Foster Rhea Dulles, *Twentieth Century America* (Boston, 1945), p. 369.
2. "News Bulletin—LIPA," *Common Sense,* May 11, 1933, p. 17.
    Common Sense, edited by Alfred M. Bingham and Selden Rodman, had been founded in December, 1932, on the principle that "a system based on competition for private profit can no longer serve the general welfare." Bingham, the son of Connecticut's Senator Hiram Bingham, and Rodman established this magazine to give expression to "fearless" writers. John Dos Passos, Stuart Chase, Robert S. Allen, A. J. Muste, Jay Lovestone, Morris Hillquit, C. Hartley Grattan, Louis Budenz, John Chamberlain, George Soule, Scott Nearing, and John T. Flynn were among those social critics who contributed to the periodical during its life span of almost twelve years.
    In April, 1933, *Common Sense* declared its "wholehearted support of the League for Independent Political Action," and announced that it would co-operate vigorously with that organization. The magazine's editorial viewpoint was virtually synonymous with the policies of LIPA and its successor organizations. The League's officers frequently published articles in the organ.—*Common Sense,* Dec. 5, 1932, pp. 2 f.; April 13, 1933, pp. 2, 17.
3. "The New Deal After Ten Weeks," *World Tomorrow,* June, 1933, pp. 418 f.
4. *Common Sense,* May 25, 1933, pp. 2 and 17. See *New Leader,* May 13, 1933, for an official Socialist report on the Continental Congress; the platform of the Congress is also reproduced in this issue.
5. *New York Times,* Feb. 6, 1933, p. 3; Feb. 12, sec. VI, pp. 1 f.
6. Theodore Saloutos and John D. Hicks, *Agricultural Discontent in the Middle West, 1900-1939* (Madison, 1951), pp. 447 ff.; *New York Times,* March 13, 1933, p. 11, May 5, p. 11.
7. Saloutos and Hicks, *op. cit.,* pp. 448 ff.; *New York Times,* May 13, 1933, p. 3.
8. Saloutos and Hicks, *op. cit.,* pp. 483 ff.; *New York Times,* Oct. 21, 1933, p. 8, November 2, p. 30.
9. Franklin D. Roosevelt Library, Simpson to Roosevelt, Oct. 24, 1933.
10. *New York Times,* Oct. 20, 1933, p. 10.
11. *Ibid.,* Oct. 26, 1933, p. 29; Nov. 2, p. 30; Nov. 5, p. 6; Nov. 6, p. 9; Nov. 7, p. 1.
12. Saloutos and Hicks, *op. cit.,* pp. 485 ff.; *New York Times,* Nov. 19, 1933, sec. IV, p. 6.
13. *The Wisconsin Dairyman's News,* Feb., 1934, p. 2.
14. George W. Norris MSS, Howard Y. Williams to Norris, March 3, 1933.
15. *Common Sense,* June 8, 1933, p. 17; July, p. 27; Aug., p. 3. It should be noted that the official position of the Continental Congress'

executive committee was that the "time [is] not ripe for a new party."—
New Leader, July 15, 1933, p. 12.

16. *Common Sense,* September, 1933, p. 27.

17. Selden Rodman, "A New Radical Party," *New Republic,* Sept. 20, 1933, pp. 151 ff.

18. *Common Sense,* Oct., 1933, p. 19.

19. Rodman, *op. cit.,* pp. 151 ff.; *Common Sense,* Oct., 1933, pp. 2 f., 27; Russel B. Nye, *Midwestern Progressive Politics* (East Lansing, 1951), p. 362.

20. *Common Sense,* Oct., 1933, pp. 2 f. and 27.
This magazine announced that it would serve as the semi-official publication of both the League for Independent Political Action and the Farmer-Labor Political Federation.

21. Oswald Garrison Villard MSS, Villard to Alfred M. Bingham, Sept. 14, 1933, and April 10, 1934.

22. *Common Sense,* Oct., 1933, p. 27; Nov., p. 28; Dec., p. 26.

23. *New York Times,* January 5, 1934, p. 5.

24. *Common Sense,* March, 1934, pp. 2 f.

25. *Ibid.,* Sept., 1934, p. 2.

26. *Ibid.,* Dec., 1933, p. 26.

27. Statement by Howard Y. Williams, personal interview, April 23, 1952; and Alfred M. Bingham, "On the Political Front," *Common Sense,* March, 1934, p. 24.

28. Statement by Thomas R. Amlie, personal interview, April 8, 1952; statement by Howard Y. Williams, personal interview, April 23, 1952.

29. *Wisconsin State Journal* (Madison), May 3-5, May 13-19, 1933, all on p. 1; Harold F. Gosnell and Morris H. Cohen, "Progressive Politics: Wisconsin an Example," *American Political Science Review,* Oct., 1940, pp. 924 f.

30. *Milwaukee Leader,* April 23, 1934, p. 1.

31. Edward N. Doan, *The La Follettes and the Wisconsin Idea* (New York, 1947), p. 178; *New York Times,* Aug. 19, 1934, p. 25.

32. Late in 1933 and early in 1934, Wisconsin political observers frequently referred to the new-party activities as "Mr. Amlie's movement."

33. Mark R. Byers, "A New La Follette Party," *North American Review,* May, 1934, pp. 407 ff.; *Milwaukee Journal,* May 20, 1934, p. 1.

34. "Progressive Party Platform," *Wisconsin Blue Book, 1935* (Madison, 1935), pp. 476 ff.

35. *New York Times,* Oct. 20, 1944, p. 13; and Nov. 7, 1935, p. 3. See also Philip F. La Follette MSS, Aldrich Revell (Assistant Secretary to Governor La Follette) to A. W. Rees, May 17, 1935.

36. *Wisconsin Blue Book, 1935,* pp. 476 ff.

37. Howard Y. Williams MSS, Thomas R. Amlie to Williams, May 20, 1934.

38. *Milwaukee Leader,* May 21, 1934, p. 2.

39. *Ibid.,* May 19, 1934, p. 8.

40. *Farmer-Labor Leader,* May 30, 1934, p. 2; Philip F. La Follette MSS, press release of a speech by Senator Lynn J. Frazier of North Dakota, in Menomonie, Wisconsin, Oct. 4, 1934; *New York Times,* Oct. 23, 1934, p. 16.

41. *The Progressive* (Madison), June 23, 1934, p. 2.

42. *Wisconsin Blue Book, 1935,* pp. 613, 437 ff., 191 ff.

43. *Sheboygan Press,* Nov. 7, 1934, p. 6.
44. *Janesville Daily Gazette,* Nov. 7, 1934, p. 6.
45. *Ibid.,* Nov. 8, 1934, p. 6.
46. *New York Times,* Dec. 9, 1934, p. 36.
47. Statement by Howard Y. Williams, personal interview, April 23, 1952; George H. Mayer, *The Political Career of Floyd B. Olson* (Minneapolis, 1951), pp. 170 ff.
48. *Farmer-Labor Leader,* March 30, 1934, pp. 4 f.
49. Mayer, *op. cit.,* p. 172.
50. *Farmer-Labor Leader,* March 30, 1934, p. 5.
51. Mayer, *op. cit.,* p. 173.
52. *New York Times,* April 8, 1934, sec. IV, pp. 1, 7.
53. Mayer, *op. cit.,* pp. 173 ff.
54. *Ibid.,* pp. 178 ff.
55. Cf. Minnesota Secretary of State, *Legislative Manual of the State of Minnesota* (Minneapolis, 1933), p. 200, with that of 1935, pp. 205, 378 f.
56. Mayer, *op. cit.,* chap. X.
57. *Ibid.,* pp. 260 ff.; *New York Times,* Oct. 28, 1934, sec. IV, pp. 1, 7; Oct. 18, p. 11; and Joseph R. Starr, "Labor and Farmer Groups and the Three Party System," *Southwestern Social Science Quarterly,* June, 1936, pp. 18 f.

III

1. Broadus Mitchell, *Depression Decade* (New York, 1947), pp. 447 f., 453.
2. *New York Times,* May 24, 1935, p. 1.
3. *Ibid.,* May 28, 1935, pp. 1 and 17, May 30, p. 1; Mitchell (see note 1), pp. 258 f., 277 f.
4. *Report of the Proceedings of the Fifty-fifth Annual Convention of the American Federation of Labor, Oct. 7-19, 1935* (Washington, 1935), pp. 22 f., 758 ff.
5. Theodore Saloutos and John D. Hicks, *Agricultural Discontent in the Middle West, 1900-1939* (Madison, 1951), pp. 497 f.; Harold F. Gosnell and Morris H. Cohen, "Progressive Politics: Wisconsin an Example," *American Political Science Review,* Oct., 1940, pp. 924 f.
6. *New York Times,* Sept. 20, 1935, p. 11, Jan. 7, 1936, p. 12, Jan. 15, p. 6; *Farmers' Equity Union News,* Jan., 1935, p. 4, Feb., p. 11.
7. *Progressive,* May 4, 1935, p. 1; *New York Times,* April 28, 1935, p. 1, April 29, p. 4; Leon Vanderlyn, "Jeffersonian Agrarianism," *New Republic,* April 3, 1935, pp. 215 f.
8. *South Dakota News,* Oct. 3, 1935, p. 5.
9. Harold F. Gosnell, *Grass Roots Politics* (Washington, 1942), p. 43.
10. *New York Times,* April 13, 1935, p. 1.
11. *Ibid.,* Aug. 30, 1934, p. 18, Aug. 31, p. 3; Russel B. Nye, *Midwestern Progressive Politics* (East Lansing, 1951), pp. 364 f.; Upton Sinclair, *E.P.I.C. Plan for California* (New York, 1934).
12. California Secretary of State, *Statement of Vote at General Election Held on November 6, 1934* (Sacramento, 1934), p. 5.
13. Philip F. La Follette MSS, Ray McKaig to Philip F. La Follette, May 17, 1935.

14. Sidney Lens, *Left, Right and Center* (Hinsdale, 1949), p. 317; Richard Neuberger, "The Northwest Goes Leftish," *New Republic,* November 7, 1934, p. 357; *New York Times,* August 25, 1935, sec. IV, p. 12; Oregon Secretary of State, *Oregon Blue Book, 1935-1936* (Salem, 1937), p. 170.

15. Harold E. Fey, "Fascism—American Style," *Fellowship,* May, 1935, pp. 6 f.

16. Franklin D. Roosevelt Library, C. B. Warner to Roosevelt, Nov. 17, 1934.

17. Harold L. Ickes, *The Secret Diary of Harold L. Ickes—The First Thousand Days* (New York, 1953), pp. 304 f., 316, 303. President Roosevelt evidently viewed the political picture with apprehension. The results of a Democratic National Committee secret poll taken in the spring of 1935 found him less popular than at any other time since assuming office. James A. Farley, *Jim Farley's Story—The Roosevelt Years* (New York, 1948), p. 54; Elliott Roosevelt (ed.), *F.D.R.—His Personal Letters, 1928-1945,* I (New York, 1950), 453 f.

18. Not only was Senator Cutting a recognized member of the progressive bloc in Congress, but, using his considerable personal fortune, he served as chief individual financial supporter of the nation's progressives. For example, the Senator's will included bequests of $50,000 and $25,000 to Robert and Philip La Follette, respectively. *New York Times,* June 30, 1935, sec. IV, p. 2.

19. Richard L. Neuberger and Stephen B. Kahn, *Integrity—The Life of George W. Norris* (New York, 1937), pp. 308 f.; *New York Times,* May 21, 1935, p. 13, June 30, sec. IV, p. 2.

20. Elliott Roosevelt (see note 17), I, 452 f.

21. Franklin D. Roosevelt Library, Farley to Roosevelt, Feb. 26, 1935.

22. Philip F. La Follette MSS, Aldrich Revell to A. M. Rees, May 17, 1935.

23. Norman Thomas, *The Choice before Us* (New York, 1934), pp. 145 ff., 81, 230 f.

24. *New York Times,* June 7, 1934, p. 5.

25. *Ibid.,* Dec. 1, 1934, p. 4; Dec. 2, p. 35; Dec. 3, p. 1; Dec. 4, pp. 6, 18; Dec. 7, p. 22.

26. *Socialist Call,* March 23, 1935, p. 2; *New York Times,* March 24, 1935, p. 12, March 25, p. 9.

27. *New York Times,* Dec. 4, 1934, p. 6. For detailed accounts of this schism see Egbert and Persons (eds.), *Socialism and American Life* (Princeton, 1952), pp. 369 ff., and David A. Shannon, *The Socialist Party of America* (New York, 1955), pp. 235 ff.

28. *New York Times,* Aug. 7, 1935, p. 4; Georgi Dimitrov, *Selected Speeches and Articles, 1935* (London, 1935), pp. 39-157, especially 114.

29. Earl Browder, "For Working Class Unity! For a Workers' and Farmers' Labor Party!", *Communist,* Sept., 1935, pp. 787 ff.

30. *United Action,* Dec. 13, 1935, p. 1.

31. Philip F. La Follette MSS, La Follette to McKaig, May 31, 1935.

32. *New York Times,* May 19, 1935, sec. VII, pp. 5 and 19; Aug. 18, 1935, sec. VII, pp. 5 and 14; May 20, 1935, p. 1; July 28, 1935, sec. II, p. 3; Oct. 13, 1935, p. 2; Oct,. 23, 1934, p. 16; Oct. 24, 1934, p. 20.

33. *Minnesota Leader,* March 23, 1935, pp. 1 and 6; Jonathan Mitchell, "Front-Fighters in Congress," *New Republic,* June 19, 1935, pp. 156 f.; statement by Howard Y. Williams, personal interview, April

23, 1952; statement by Thomas R. Amlie, personal interview, April 8, 1952.

34. Howard Y. Williams MSS, Amlie to Williams, Nov. 15, 1934.

35. *Ibid.,* Williams to Amlie, Nov. 9, 1934.

36. *St. Paul Pioneer Press,* Dec. 9, 1934, pp. 1 and 8; *New York Times,* Dec. 9, 1934, p. 36.

37. *New York Times,* Dec. 10, 1934, p. 5.

38. *Ibid.,* May 5, 1935, p. 33.

39. Philip F. La Follette MSS, Amlie, Marcantonio, Lundeen, Scott and Schneider to La Follette, June 11, 1935.

40. Despite this use of two designations, the movement hereafter will be referred to as the American Commonwealth Political Federation.

41. *Chicago Tribune,* July 6, 1935, p. 2, July 7, p. 13; *New York Times,* June 30, 1935, sec. II, p. 2, July 6, p. 1, July 7, pp. 1, 21; *New Republic,* July 24, 1935, pp. 292 f. See Robert Morss Lovett, "A Party in Embryo," *New Republic,* July 24, 1935, pp. 295 ff., for the complete text of the ACPF platform.

42. Russel B. Nye, *Midwestern Progressive Politics, 1870-1950* (East Lansing, 1951), p. 368.

43. *Los Angeles Evening Post Record,* July 5, 1935, p. 1.

44. *New York Times,* July 8, 1935, p. 14.

45. *Socialist Call,* July 13, 1935, pp. 1, 4; *New York Times,* Oct. 14, 1935, p. 5.

46. *New Republic,* July 24, 1935, pp. 292 f.

47. *Nation,* July 17, 1935, pp. 57 f.

48. *Boise Valley Herald,* July 25, 1935, p. 3.

49. *New York Times,* July 19, 1935, p. 2.

50. *Christian Century,* July 17, 1935, p. 932.

IV

1. (New York, 1935).

2. *Ibid., passim.*

3. (New York, 1935).

4. *Ibid.,* p. 281.

5. *Ibid.,* pp. 275 f.

6. *Ibid.,* chap. XIV.

7. (New York, 1934).

8. (New York, 1935 and 1938).

9. *Ibid.,* p. 47.

10. *Ibid.,* p. 73.

11. *Ibid.,* pp. 196 ff.

12. *Ibid.,* p. 5.

13. *Ibid., passim.* In addition to the volumes above mentioned, see also Harold Loeb, *Production for Use* (New York, 1936) and Thomas R. Amlie, *Forgotten Man's Handbook* (Madison, 1935 and 1936). These inexpensive books probably would have served as two of the chief pieces of campaign literature for any 1936 farmer-labor party.

14. Thomas R. Amlie, "The American Commonwealth Federation— What Chance in 1936?" *Common Sense,* Aug., 1935, pp. 6 f.

15. *New York Times,* Aug. 21, 1935, p. 20.

16. *Ibid.,* Aug. 28, 1935, p. 5; Aug. 29, p. 1.

17. *Ibid.,* Sept. 7, 1935, p. 1.

18. Howard Y. Williams MSS, Press Release of Thomas R. Amlie, Sept. 7, 1935.
19. *New York Times*, Aug. 25, 1935, sec. IV, p. 12; *Common Sense*, Oct., 1935, p. 4; *New Republic*, May 8, 1935, p. 353; Philip F. La Follette MSS, Amlie to La Follette, July 6, 1936, enclosing "a list of some of our best workers in behalf of a third party movement."
20. *Milwaukee Leader*, Dec. 2, 1935, pp. 1 f.; *Capital Times*, Dec. 2, 1935, pp. 1, 8; *Kenosha Labor*, Dec. 6, 1935, p. 6.
21. Floyd B. Olson MSS, Press Release of Floyd B. Olson, Jan. 4, 1935.
22. *Ibid.*, J. H. Hay to Vince A. Day, Aug. 17, 1935.
23. Hulda F. Humola, "The Farmer-Labor Party in Minnesota, 1930-1938" (unpublished master's dissertation, University of Chicago, 1944), pp. 131 ff.
24. *New York Times*, Nov. 16, 1935, pp. 1 f. Governor Olson discussed his political and economic ideas at some length in the pages of *Common Sense*; see especially, Floyd B. Olson, "Why a New National Party?" *Common Sense*, Jan., 1936, pp. 6 ff.
25. *New York Times*, Nov. 17, 1935, p. 29.
26. Floyd B. Olson MSS, Bingham to Olson, Feb. 18, 1936.
27. *Ibid.*
28. *New Republic*, April 1, 1936, pp. 208 f.
29. *Nation*, April 15, 1936, pp. 468 f.
30. *Common Sense*, March, 1936, p. 25.
31. *Ibid.*, April, 1936, p. 2.
32. *Ibid.*, p. 23.
33. *New York Times*, Dec. 13, 1935, p. 14 and March 24, 1936, p. 2.
34. *Ibid.*, March 6, 1936, p. 9. The Communist national daily newspaper publicized the "need" for a farmer-labor party throughout the spring of 1936; for a pungent example, see Earl Browder's column in *Sunday Worker*, May 17, 1936, p. 5.
35. *New York Times*, March 12, 1936, p. 18. The health of Floyd B. Olson, who had previously been mentioned as a possible new-party presidential candidate, had been deteriorating since 1934. The governor died of cancer on Aug. 22, 1936. See George H. Mayer, *The Political Career of Floyd B. Olson* (Minneapolis, 1951), pp. 289 ff.
36. *Minnesota Leader*, April 4, 1936, p. 3; *New York Times*, March 28, 1936, p. 2, March 29, pp. 1, 26; *St. Paul Pioneer Press*, March 27, 1936, p. 3.
37. *Minnesota Leader*, April 18, 1936, p. 1; May 9, p. 1.
38. *New York Times*, May 6, 1936, p. 23.
39. Frederick Rudolph, "The American Liberty League, 1934-1940," *American Historical Review*, Oct., 1950, pp. 19 ff.
40. Franklin D. Roosevelt Library, Memorandum to the President from Labor's Non-Partisan League, June 22, 1936. The League was led by George Berry and John L. Lewis, and was representative of the most liberal elements of the labor movement.
41. Mayer (see note 35), p. 297.
42. *New York Times*, May 25, 1936, p. 2.
43. Statement by Thomas R. Amlie, personal interview, April 8, 1952; statement by Howard Y. Williams, personal interview, April 23, 1952; *New York Times*, May 31, 1936, p. 26; *Minnesota Leader*, May 30, 1936, p. 1.
44. *New York Times*, May 31, 1936, p. 26; June 1, p. 2.

45. *Minnesota Leader,* May 30, 1936, p. 4.
46. *New York Times,* May 31, 1936, p. 26, June 1, p. 2; statement by Howard Y. Williams, personal interview, April 23, 1952.
47. *New York Times,* June 1, 1936, p. 2; *Nation,* July 18, 1936, sec. II.
48. Thomas, *After the New Deal, What?* (New York, 1936), pp. 206 ff.; *Socialist Call,* June 6, 1936, p. 12.
49. *Daily Worker,* June 3, 1936, p. 2; Earl Browder, *Democracy or Fascism: Report to the Ninth Convention of the Communist Party* (New York, 1936), pp. 11 f.
50. Franklin D. Roosevelt Library, Melvin D. Hildreth to James A. Farley, Sept. 14, 1936; statement by Howard Y. Williams, personal interview, April 23, 1952; *Common Sense,* Oct., 1936, p. 3.

V

1. Selden Rodman, "The Insurgent Line-up for 1936," *American Mercury,* May, 1935, pp. 77 ff.
2. *New York Times,* April 23, 1935, p. 8.
3. *Ibid.,* June 28, 1936, p. 25.
4. Sidney Lens, *Left, Right and Center* (Hinsdale, 1949), p. 283.
5. Henry G. Teigan MSS, Teigan to W. A. Weber, Jan. 8, 1936.
6. *New York Times,* Aug. 19, 1936, p. 14.
7. *Wisconsin Blue Book, 1937* (Madison, 1937), p. 419.
8. Miscellaneous letters in the Roosevelt Library from Coughlin to Roosevelt or to his secretary, Marvin McIntyre.
9. *New York Times,* Nov. 28, 1933, p. 17.
10. *Ibid.,* Jan. 17, 1934, p. 14.
11. *Ibid.,* Jan. 19, 1934, p. 7.
12. *Ibid.,* Nov. 19, 1934, p. 25; *Social Justice,* March 13, 1936, p. 1.
13. Quoted, with some editing, from *Social Justice,* March 13, 1936, p. 7, and Charles E. Coughlin, *A Series of Lectures on Social Justice, 1934-1935* (Royal Oak, 1935), pp. 17 f.
14. Harold F. Gosnell, *Grass Roots Politics* (Washington, 1942), pp. 114 ff.; V. O. Key, Jr., *Southern Politics* (New York, 1949), pp. 157 ff.; Gerald L. K. Smith, "How Come Huey Long?—Bogeyman—or Superman?" *New Republic,* Feb. 13, 1935, p. 15; Allan Sindler, *Huey Long's Louisiana* (Baltimore, 1956), pp. 45 ff.; Reinhard Luthin, *American Demagogues—Twentieth Century* (Boston, 1954), chap. X.
15. Allan Sindler, *op. cit.,* p. 84. For an extended discussion of the nation's problems by Huey Long, see his *Every Man a King* (New Orleans, 1933).
16. *Ibid.,* pp. 85 f.
17. *New York Times,* Jan. 8, 1935, pp. 1, 4.
18. *Ibid.,* Jan. 10, 1935, p. 1.
19. *Ibid.,* March 4, 1935, p. 2; Coughlin, *Series of Lectures, 1934-1935,* pp. 193 ff.
20. *Ibid.,* March 5, 1935, p. 1.
21. *Ibid.,* March 7, 1935, p. 4; March 8, p. 1.
22. *Ibid.,* March 13, 1935, p. 11; James Farley, *Jim Farley's Story—The Roosevelt Years* (New York, 1948), p. 52.
23. *New York Times,* March 24, 1935, p. 12; March 25, p. 9; March 6, p. 7; April 3, p. 3; April 8, p. 11.
24. *Ibid.,* March 15, 1935, p. 4; April 9, p. 11; April 25, p. 2.

NOTES (pp.127-145)

25. *Ibid.*, April 28, 1935, p. 1; May 6, p. 2; May 22, p. 10; June 14, p. 14.
26. Farley (see note 22), pp. 51 f.
27. *New York Times*, Aug. 14, 1935, p. 13.
28. *Ibid.*, Sept. 10, 1935, p. 1, Sept. 11, p. 17, Sept. 20, p. 1, Sept. 22, sec. IV, p. 11; Franklin D. Roosevelt Library, telegram from Smith to Roosevelt, Sept. 17, 1935.
29. Gosnell, p. 120; Herbert Harris, "That Third Party," *Current History*, Oct., 1936, pp. 82-84; Sindler, *op. cit.*, pp. 119 ff.
30. Harris (see note 29), pp. 82 ff.
31. It was estimated by Coughlin's newspaper that from twelve to fifteen million persons listened to his Sunday radio program. *Social Justice*, March 13, 1936, p. 1.
32. Charles E. Coughlin, *A Series of Lectures on Social Justice, 1935-1936* (Royal Oak, 1936), p. 8.
33. *Ibid.*, p. 10.
34. *Ibid.*, p. 46.
35. *Ibid.*, pp. 126 ff., 39, 41.
36. *Ibid.*, pp. 14 f., 20 f.
37. *Ibid.*, pp. 13, 9.
38. Farley, p. 52.
39. *New York Times*, Dec. 10, 1935, p. 13; Dec. 13, p. 24. It should be indicated that a number of prominent Catholic leaders, including William Cardinal O'Connell of Boston and Monsignor John A. Ryan of the Catholic University, had been critical of Coughlin's activities for a number of years, although their comments were not circulated widely.
40. William K. Mason, *Townsend plus Coughlin Equals Power* (Malden, 1936), pp. 5, 17 ff. Hadley Cantril, *The Psychology of Social Movements* (New York, 1941), chap. VII.
41. Franklin D. Roosevelt Library, S. High to Stephen Early, Aug. 29, 1935; M. F. Smith to J. Farley, Oct. 21, 1935; J. G. Winant to Roosevelt, Dec. 4, 1935.
42. Broadus Mitchell, *Depression Decade* (New York, 1947), pp. 306 ff.
43. *New York Times*, Dec. 13, 1935, p. 14; Dec. 15, pp. 1, 39; Dec. 17, p. 13; Dec. 18, p. 1.
44. *Ibid.*, March 24, 1936, p. 2.
45. *Ibid.*, May 5, 1936, p. 10; May 29, p. 2.
46. Franklin D. Roosevelt Library, Townsend Club # 13, Spokane, Washington, to Roosevelt, June 1, 1936.
47. *New York Times*, May 23, 1936, p. 9; *Social Justice*, May 29, 1936, p. 7.
48. *Social Justice*, May 8, 1936, pp. 1, 9; May 22, pp. 1, 9.
49. *New York Times*, June 17, 1936, p. 1.
50. *Ibid.*, June 18, 1936, p. 3; June 19, p. 7.
51. *Social Justice*, June 22, 1936, pp. 14 f.
52. *Ibid.*, p. 6.
53. *New York Times*, June 20, 1936, pp. 1 ff., June 26, p. 11; *Social Justice*, June 22, 1936, p. 5, June 29, p. 1.
54. Harris, pp. 80 ff.
55. *New York Times*, June 28, 1936, p. 25; June 30, p. 4.
56. *Ibid.*, July 2, 1936, p. 6; July 3, p. 4.
57. *Ibid.*, June 21, 1936, p. 1.

207

58. Elliott Roosevelt (ed.), *F.D.R.—His Personal Letters, 1928-1945,* I (New York, 1950), 602.

59. *New York Times,* June 22, 1936, p. 1; July 19, sec. IV, p. 3; Oct. 2, p. 1.

60. Earl Browder, *Democracy or Fascism: Report to the Ninth Annual Convention of the Communist Party* (New York, 1936), p. 19; Norman Thomas, *After the New Deal, What?* (New York, 1936), pp. 5 f.; *Nation,* July 11, 1936, pp. 34 ff., June 27, p. 828; *New Republic,* July 1, 1936, p. 226; *St. Paul Pioneer Press,* June 20, 1936, p. 3; *Common Sense,* Oct., 1936, pp. 3 f., 33.

61. *Vital Speeches of the Day,* July 1, 1936, pp. 615 f.

62. *New York Times,* July 7, 1936, p. 14; *Social Justice,* July 6, 1936, p. 5, Oct. 12, p. 2.

63. Harris, pp. 80 ff.

64. *Social Justice,* June 29, 1936, p. 2; Sept. 28, p. 15.

65. Harris, pp. 80 ff.

66. Franklin D. Roosevelt Library, Sheehy to Marguerite LeHand, June 18, 1936.

67. *Ibid.,* Mahoney to Roosevelt, July 21, 1936; *New York Times,* Sept. 18, 1936, p. 13, Sept. 26, p. 1.

68. *New York Times,* Oct. 12, 1936, p. 18; Oct. 13, p. 24.

69. *Ibid.,* Sept. 26, 1936, p. 1; Oct. 13, p. 24.

70. *Ibid.,* April 2, 1936, p. 9, April 10, p. 14; Labor's Non-Partisan League, *Labor's Non-Partisan League: Its Origin and Growth* (Washington, 1939), p. 4.

71. Stephen B. Sarasohn, "The Struggle for Control of the American Labor Party, 1936-1948" (unpublished Master's thesis, Columbia University, 1948), pp. 8, 20 f.

72. Lens, pp. 316 f.

73. *Progressive,* Sept. 19, 1936, p. 6; Progressive National Committee Supporting Franklin D. Roosevelt for President, *Declaration of Principles* (New York, 1936), pp. 1 ff.

74. Robert M. La Follette, Jr., *Progressivism is Americanism* (New York, 1936), *passim.*

75. Donald R. McCoy, "The Progressive National Committee of 1936," *Western Political Quarterly,* June, 1956, pp. 464, 466 f.

76. *New York Times,* Oct. 18, 1936, sec. IV, p. 6; Oct. 28, p. 24.

77. United States Department of Commerce, *Historical Statistics of the United States, 1789-1945* (Washington, 1949), p. 288; Samuel Lubell, *The Future of American Politics* (New York, 1952), pp. 141 ff.

78. Murray S. and Susan W. Stedman, *Discontent at the Polls* (New York, 1950), p. 177; *Wisconsin Blue Book, 1937,* p. 419.

79. *Superior Evening Telegram,* Nov. 18, 1936, p. 6.

VI

1. *Common Sense,* January, 1937, p. 24.

2. Philip F. La Follette MSS, Gordon Sinykin to Fred Bettelheim, Jr., Nov. 11, 1936.

3. Minnesota Farmer-Labor Association MSS, Ernest Lundeen to the Chairman of the Association's State Convention, Jan. 28, 1937; minutes of the Executive Committee Meeting, July 17, 1937.

4. Sidney Lens, *Left, Right and Center* (Hinsdale, 1949), pp. 318 f.; *New York Times,* Oct. 1, 1936, p. 13, Oct. 23, 1936, p. 15.

5. *New York Times,* Nov. 12, 1936, p. 3, Nov. 7, pp. 1, 8, Feb. 1, 1937, p. 1; John L. Lewis, "The Struggle for Industrial Democracy," *Common Sense,* March, 1937, pp. 8 ff.

6. *New York Times,* Nov. 6, 1936, p. 6, Nov. 24, p. 16; Earl Browder, *The People's Front* (New York, 1938); Hadley Cantril and Mildred Strunk (eds.), *Public Opinion, 1935-1946* (Princeton, 1951), p. 576.

7. *New York Times,* Aug. 21, 1937, p. 1; Aug. 24, p. 14; Nov. 7, sec. IV, p. 7.

8. John L. Lewis, pp. 5 ff.; *New York Times,* Aug. 21, 1937, p. 1, Aug. 28, p. 3, Sept. 4, p. 1.

9. *New York Times,* March 1, 1937, p. 1; March 2, p. 1.

10. In late 1937 and early 1938, disgruntlement and disillusionment characterized commentaries on the national administration's recession policies and defeats in Congress in liberal periodicals like the *New Republic, Nation, Christian Century,* and *Common Sense.* These attitudes were also mentioned or reflected in the later writings of some of President Roosevelt's associates in their discussions of the period. See James A. Farley, *Jim Farley's Story: The Roosevelt Years* (New York, 1948), pp. 91-150; Harold L. Ickes, *The Secret Diary of Harold L. Ickes—The Inside Struggle* (New York, 1954), pp. 260-340; Frances Perkins, *The Roosevelt I Knew* (New York, 1946), p. 302; Samuel I. Rosenman, *Working with Roosevelt* (New York, 1952), pp. 169, 181.

11. Arthur A. Ekirch, Jr., *The Civilian and the Military* (New York, 1956), pp. 246-51.

12. Philip F. La Follette MSS, P. La Follette to Edwin Hadfield, Jr., Oct. 7, 1937.

13. Statement by P. La Follette, personal interview, April 4, 1952.

14. Franklin D. Roosevelt Library, Otto La Budde to James A. Farley, July 20, 1936; *Capital Times,* March 2, 1938, p. 1.

15. P. La Follette MSS, P. La Follette to Hadfield, Oct. 7, 1937; statement by P. La Follette, personal interview, April 4, 1952.

16. *Capital Times,* May 19, 1937, pp. 1, 8.

17. P. La Follette MSS, "La Follette Speech at Riverview Park, Des Moines," July 31, 1937.

18. *Omaha World Herald,* Sept. 7, 1937, p. 7.

19. P. La Follette MSS, Paul H. Douglas to P. La Follette, July 16, 1937; La Follette to Douglas, July 19; Douglas to La Follette, July 21; and La Follette to Douglas, Aug. 2; La Follette to John R. Richards, Aug. 11; Richards to La Follette, Nov. 26; La Follette to Richards, Dec. 15.

20. P. La Follette MSS, John F. Wirds to P. La Follette, Sept. 17, 1937; P. La Follette to Wirds, Sept. 20; H. P. Fagan to Gordon Sinykin, Sept. 12.

21. *Capital Times,* April 21, 1938, pp. 3, 10; *New York Times,* April 21, 1938, p. 3.

22. *New York Times,* April 22, 1938, p. 4; April 23, p. 2.

23. *Ibid.,* April 25, 1938, p. 7; *Capital Times,* April 25, 1938, p. 1.

24. *New York Times,* April 26, 1938, p. 5.

25. The cross-and-circle symbol was seen by Governor La Follette as representing the unity of the nation, the power of the ballot, equality, and the need for multiplication of wealth and organized social action. Many people, undoubtedly to the detriment of the National Progressives, likened the emblem to Nazi and Fascist insignia. *Life* reproduced the symbol under a half-page photograph of La Follette

209

standing on a podium with his hand held up as if in the act of giving a Nazi salute (*Life*, May 9, 1938, p. 9).

26. Russel B. Nye, *Midwestern Progressive Politics, 1870-1950* (East Lansing, 1951), p. 372.

27. P. La Follette MSS, "For Release, Thursday, April 28, at 8 P.M., Speech by Philip F. La Follette." For a printed version in pamphlet form see Philip La Follette, *A New Movement . . . The National Progressives of America . . . Is Under Way* (Madison, 1938).

28. *New York Times*, May 29, 1938, sec. IV, p. 10; Cantril and Strunk (eds.) (see note 6), p. 577.

29. *New York Times*, April 30, 1938, p. 3.

30. *Ibid.*, May 2, 1938, p. 17.

31. *Farmers' Equity Union News*, May, 1938, p. 2.

32. *New York Times*, May 1, 1938, sec. II, p. 6.

33. *New Republic*, May 4, 1938, pp. 382 f.; May 11, 1938, pp. 3 f.

34. *Common Sense*, June, 1938, p. 3.

35. *Christian Century*, May 11, 1938, p. 8.

36. *Nation*, April 30, 1938, pp. 492 f.; May 7, 1938, pp. 519 f.

37. *New York Times*, April 30, 1938, p. 3; May 4, p. 11; May 12, p. 12.

38. *Minnesota Leader*, May 7, 1938, p. 4; Minnesota Farmer-Labor Association MSS, Minutes of the Minnesota Farmer-Labor Association's State Committee, May 21, 1938.

39. *Socialist Call*, April 30, 1938, p. 5.

40. *New York Times*, May 15, 1938, p. 2.

41. See Central Committee, Communist Party, U.S.A., *The La Follette Third Party* (New York, 1938).

42. *New York Times*, April 30, 1938, p. 3.

43. *Common Sense*, June, 1938, p. 23.

44. Franklin D. Roosevelt Library, miscellaneous memoranda, n.d., President's File and Papers of the Democratic National Committee.

45. Ickes, *op. cit., The Inside Struggle*, p. 379.

46. Elliott Roosevelt (ed.), *F.D.R.: His Personal Letters, 1928-1945* (New York, 1950), II, 785.

47. *Capital Times*, April 29, 1938, p. 1, April 30, pp. 1, 3, May 1, p. 1; *New York Times*, May 1, 1938, p. 1.

48. *New York Times*, Sept. 25, 1938, sec. IV, p. 7.

49. *Statement of Vote at Primary Election Held on August 30, 1938 in the State of California* (Sacramento, 1938), pp. 5 f.

50. Statement by P. La Follette, personal interview, April 4, 1952.

51. *Capital Times*, April 28, 1938, p. 1. The editor of the *Capital Times*, William T. Evjue, also served as editor of the *Progressive*, the official newspaper of the Wisconsin Progressive party. While the *Progressive's* editorials supported the National Progressive program, its pages devoted very little space to news coverage of the organization.

52. *Capital Times*, May 1, 1938, p. 26.

53. *Ibid.*, May 22, 1938, p. 1.

54. *Ibid.*, May 25, 1938, p. 1; *Janesville Daily Gazette*, May 25, 1938, p. 1.

55. *Capital Times*, October 19, 1937, p. 20. For La Follette's discussion of the problems of legislative procedure, see his *Democracy Functions in Wisconsin: A Record of Achievement of the 1937 Legislature* (Madison, 1937), pp. 7 f.

NOTES (pp. 179-197)

56. Evjue explained the reasons for his editorial attacks on his party in a personal letter to James A. Stone, Dec. 14, 1937. Papers of James A. Stone (State Historical Society of Wisconsin).
57. William F. Raney, *Wisconsin: A Story of Progress* (New York, 1940), p. 369.
58. *Wisconsin Blue Book, 1940* (Madison, 1940), pp. 606 ff. A substitute Democratic candidate for governor, Harry W. Bolens, received only 78,446 votes, which illustrated the appeal of the coalition idea. It is also interesting to note that Governor La Follette received 38 per cent of the ballots cast for governor in 1938 as compared with 39 per cent in 1934 and 46 per cent in 1936. Compare the *Wisconsin Blue Book* for 1940 (p. 606) with those of 1935 (p. 613) and 1937 (p. 420).
59. *Statement of Vote at General Election Held on November 8, 1938, in the State of California* (Sacramento, 1938), p. 4.
60. *Official Register, 1939-1940* (Des Moines, 1939), pp. 571 ff.
61. *Capital Times,* Nov. 9, 1938, p. 12.

VII

1. George W. Norris, *Fighting Liberal: The Autobiography of George W. Norris* (New York, 1945), p. 353.
2. Rudolf Heberle, *Social Movements* (New York, 1951), p. 93.
3. See Ruth S. Cavan and Katherine H. Ranck, *The Family and the Depression* (Chicago, 1938).
4. Hadley Cantril, *The Psychology of Social Movements* (New York, 1941), p. 177.
5. *Ibid.,* pp. 37 ff.
6. Heberle, *op. cit.,* pp. 174 ff. A good illustration of American refusal to accept class reality is seen in the results of an American Institute of Public Opinion poll released April 2, 1939. This survey revealed that 35 per cent of those polled ranked themselves with a social group higher than the economic group with which they were identified. See Cantril (note 4, above), p. 176.
7. Paul Douglas, *The Coming of a New Party* (New York, 1932), pp. 121, 173.
8. See Murray and Susan Stedman, *Discontent at the Polls* (New York, 1950), especially chap. X, for a recent discussion of this tradition in the United States.
9. Samuel Lubell, *The Future of American Politics* (New York, 1951), pp. 184 f.
10. Statement by Howard Y. Williams, personal interview, April 23, 1952.
11. Hugh A. Bone, "Small Political Parties, Casualties of War," *National Municipal Review,* Nov., 1943, pp. 524 ff.; Morton S. Goldstein, "The New Party and the Ballot," *New Republic,* June 3, 1936, pp. 99 f.; and William E. Hannan (ed.), *Provisions of the Laws of the Various States with Respect to the Formation of a New Political Party* (Chicago, 1938), p. 3.
12. T. V. Smith MSS, Ernest Lundeen and Hjalmar Peterson to T. V. Smith, May 29, 1936.
13. Selig Adler, *The Isolationist Impulse: Its Twentieth-Century Reaction* (London and New York, 1958), pp. 251 f.

BIBLIOGRAPHY

Books

Adler, Selig. *The Isolationist Impulse: Its Twentieth-Century Reaction.* London and New York, 1958.

American Federation of Labor. *Report of the Proceedings of the Fifty-Fourth Annual Convention, October 1-12, 1934.* Washington, 1934.
——. *Report of the Proceedings of the Fifty-fifth Annual Convention, October 7-19, 1935.* Washington, 1935.

Amlie, Thomas R. *Forgotten Man's Handbook.* Madison, 1936.

Bingham, Alfred M. *Insurgent Democracy.* New York, 1935.
—— and Selden Rodman, eds. *Challenge to the New Deal.* New York, 1934.

Browder, Earl. *Democracy or Fascism: Report to the Ninth Convention of the Communist Party.* New York, 1936.
——. *The Popular Front.* New York, 1938.

Cantril, Hadley. *The Psychology of Social Movements.* New York, 1941.

Cavan, Ruth S. and Ranck, Katherine H. *The Family and the Depression.* Chicago, 1938.

Communist Party, U.S.A. Central Committee. *The La Follette Third Party.* New York, 1938.

Conference of Progressives. *Proceedings of a Conference of Progressives, March 11 and 12, 1931.* Washington, 1931.

Coughlin, Charles E. *A Series of Lectures on Social Justice, 1934-1935.* Royal Oak, Michigan, 1935.
——. *A Series of Lectures on Social Justice, 1935-1936.* Royal Oak, Michigan, 1936.

Dewey, John. *Liberalism and Social Action.* New York, 1935.

Dimitrov, Georgi. *Selected Speeches and Articles, 1935.* London, 1935.

Doan, Edward N. *The La Follettes and the Wisconsin Idea.* New York, 1947.

Douglas, Paul H. *The Coming of a New Party.* New York, 1932.
——. *Controlling Depressions.* New York, 1935.

Egbert, Donald D. and Persons, Stow, eds. *Socialism and American Life.* 2 vols. Princeton, 1952.

Fairchild, Henry Pratt. *Profits or Prosperity?* New York, 1932.

Farley, James A. *Jim Farley's Story: The Roosevelt Years.* New York, 1948.

Gosnell, Harold F. *Grass Roots Politics.* Washington, 1942.

Hannan, William E., ed. *Provisions of the Laws of the Various States with Respect to the Formation of a New Political Party.* Chicago, 1938.

Heberle, Rudolf. *Social Movements.* New York, 1951.

Hillquit, Morris. *Should the American Workers Form a Political Party of Their Own?* New York, 1932.

Ickes, Harold L. *The Secret Diary of Harold L. Ickes: The First Thousand Days.* New York, 1953.
——. *The Secret Diary of Harold L. Ickes: The Inside Struggle.* New York, 1954.

Key, V. O., Jr. *Southern Politics.* New York, 1949.

BIBLIOGRAPHY

Labor's Non-Partisan League. *Labor's Non-Partisan League: Its Origin and Growth*. Washington, 1939.

La Follette, Philip F. *Democracy Functions in Wisconsin: a Record of Achievement of the 1937 Legislature*. Madison, 1937.

——. *A New Movement . . . The National Progressives of America . . . Is Under Way*. Madison, 1938.

La Follette, Robert M., Jr. *Progressivism is Americanism*. New York, 1936.

Laidler, Harry W. *A Program for Modern America*. New York, 1936.

——. *Toward a Farmer-Labor Party*. New York, 1938.

League for Independent Political Action. *Wanted: A New Political Alignment*. New York, 1930.

Lee, Alfred M. and Elizabeth B., eds. *The Fine Art of Propaganda: A Study of Father Coughlin's Speeches*. New York, 1939.

Lemke, William. *You and Your Money*. Philadelphia, 1937.

Lens, Sidney. *Left, Right and Center*. Hinsdale, 1949.

Loeb, Harold. *Production for Use*. New York, 1936.

——, et al. *The Chart of Plenty*. New York, 1935.

Long, Huey. *Every Man a King*. New Orleans, 1933.

Lubell, Samuel. *The Future of American Politics*. New York, 1952.

Luthin, Reinhard. *American Demagogues: Twentieth Century*. Boston, 1954.

Mason, William K. *Towsend plus Coughlin Equals Power*. Malden, 1936.

Mayer, George H. *The Political Career of Floyd B. Olson*. Minneapolis, 1951.

Mitchell, Broadus. *Depression Decade*. New York, 1947.

Neuberger, Richard and Kahn, Stephen. *Integrity: The Life of George W. Norris*. New York, 1937.

Norris, George W. *Fighting Liberal: The Autobiography of George W. Norris*. New York, 1945.

Nye, Russel B. *Midwestern Progressive Politics*. East Lansing, 1951.

Page, Kirby. *Individualism and Socialism*. New York, 1933.

Progressive National Committee Supporting Franklin D. Roosevelt for President. *Declaration of Principles*. New York, 1936.

Raney, William F. *Wisconsin, A Story of Progress*. New York, 1940.

Roosevelt, Elliott, ed. *F.D.R.: His Personal Letters, 1928-1945*. 2 vols. New York, 1950.

Rosenman, Samuel I. *Working with Roosevelt*. New York, 1952.

Saloutos, Theodore and Hicks, John D. *Agricultural Discontent in the Middle West, 1900-1939*. Madison, 1951.

Shannon, David A. *The Socialist Party of America*. New York, 1955.

Sinclair, Upton. *E.P.I.C. Plan for California*. New York, 1935.

——. *I, Candidate for Governor, and How I Got Licked*. Pasadena, 1935.

Sindler, Allan P. *Huey Long's Louisiana*. Baltimore, 1956.

Stedman, Murray S., Jr. and Susan W. *Discontent at the Polls*. New York, 1950.

Thomas, Norman. *After the New Deal, What?* New York, 1936.

——. *As I See It*. New York, 1932.

——. *The Choice before Us*. New York, 1934.

Townsend, Francis E. and Clements, Robert E. *The Townsend Plan*. Washington, 1935.

BIBLIOGRAPHY

Personal Interviews

Thomas R. Amlie, April 8, 1952.
William T. Evjue, April 10, 1952.
Philip F. La Follette, April 4, 1952.
Robert M. La Follette, Jr., April 3, 1952.
Howard Y. Williams, April 23 and 24, 1952.

Magazine Articles

Allen, Devere. "A Progressive for Revolt." *Nation*, July 27, 1932, pp. 80 ff.
Amlie, Thomas R. "The American Commonwealth Federation—What Chance in 1936?" *Common Sense*, August, 1935, pp. 6 ff.
Bingham, Alfred M. "On the Political Front." *Common Sense*, March, 1934, pp. 24 f.
Bone, Hugh A. "Small Political Parties, Casualties of War," *National Municipal Review*, November, 1943, pp. 524 ff.
Browder, Earl. "For Working Class Unity! For a Workers' and Farmers' Labor Party!" *Communist*, September, 1935, pp. 787 ff.
Byers, Mark R. "A New La Follette Party." *North American Review*, May, 1934, pp. 404 ff.
Chevalier, H. M. "Farmer-Labor Conference." *New Republic*, June 17, 1936, p. 172.
Coughlin, Charles E. "The Union Party." *Vital Speeches of the Day*, July 1, 1936, pp. 614 ff.
Dewey, John. "Prospects for a Third Party." *New Republic*, July 27, 1932, pp. 278 ff.
Douglas, Paul H. "The New Deal After Ten Weeks." *World Tomorrow*, June, 1933, pp. 418 f.
———. "Prospects for a New Political Alignment." *American Political Science Review*, November, 1931, pp. 906 ff.
Fey, Harold E. "Fascism—American Style." *Fellowship*, May, 1935, pp. 6 f.
Gard, Wayne. "The Farmers' Rebellion." *Nation*, September 7, 1932, pp. 207 ff.
Goldstein, Morton S. "The New Party and the Ballot." *New Republic*, June 3, 1936, pp. 99 f.
Gosnell, Harold F. and Cohen, Morris H. "Progressive Politics: Wisconsin an Example." *American Political Science Review*, October, 1940, pp. 921 ff.
Groves, Harold M. "Wisconsin's New Party." *Nation*, August 1, 1934, pp. 123 f.
Harris, Herbert. "That Third Party." *Current History*, October, 1936, pp. 77 ff.
Johnson, Scott D. "The Socialists and La Follette Progressivism." *Institute of Social Studies Bulletin* (Rand School), winter, 1952, pp. 87 and 94.
Leach, William. "The L.I.P.A. Cleveland Conference." *Christian Century*, July 20, 1932, p. 917.
Lerner, Max. "Third Party for 1940?" *Nation*, September 4, 1937, pp. 234 f.
Lewis, John L. "The Struggle for Industrial Democracy." *Common Sense*, March, 1937, pp. 5 ff.

Lovett, Robert Morss. "April Hopes in Madison." *New Republic,* May 11, 1938, pp. 13 f.
———. "A Party in Embryo." *New Republic,* July 24, 1935, pp. 295 ff.
———. "Progressives at Cleveland." *New Republic,* July 20, 1932, pp. 258 f.
McCoy, Donald R. "The Progressive National Committee of 1936." *Western Political Quarterly,* June, 1956, pp. 454 ff.
Neuberger, Richard. "The Northwest Goes Leftish." *New Republic,* November 7, 1934, pp. 357 f.
Olson, Floyd B. "Why a New National Party?" *Common Sense,* January, 1936, pp. 6 ff.
Rodman, Selden. "The Insurgent Line-up for 1936." *American Mercury,* May, 1935, pp. 77 ff.
———. "A New Radical Party." *New Republic,* September 20, 1933, pp. 151 ff.
Rudolph, Frederick. "The American Liberty League, 1934-1940." *American Historical Review,* October, 1950, pp. 19 ff.
Sayre, Wallace S. "Left Turn in Wisconsin." *New Republic,* May 4, 1938, pp. 300 f.
Smith, Gerald L. K. "How Come Huey Long? Bogeyman—or Superman?" *New Republic,* February 13, 1935, pp. 14 f.
Starr, Joseph R. "Labor and Farmer Groups and the Three Party System." *Southwestern Social Science Quarterly,* June, 1936, pp. 18 ff.
Thomas, Norman. "The Future of the Socialist Party." *Nation,* December 14, 1932, pp. 584 ff.
Williams, Howard Y. "Do Americans Want a New Party?" *World Tomorrow,* July, 1930, pp. 294 ff.
———. "Mr. Thomas and the LIPA." *Nation,* February 1, 1935, p. 122.

MANUSCRIPT SOURCES

Philip F. La Follette MSS, Wisconsin Historical Society.
Minnesota Farmer-Labor Association MSS, Minnesota Historical Society.
George W. Norris MSS, Library of Congress.
Floyd B. Olson MSS, Minnesota Historical Society.
General Correspondence Files, Franklin D. Roosevelt Library.
Thomas V. Smith MSS, University of Chicago Archives and Manuscript Collection.
James A. Stone MSS, Wisconsin Historical Society.
Henry G. Teigan MSS, Minnesota Historical Society.
Oswald Garrison Villard MSS, Houghton Library, Harvard University.
Howard Y. Williams MSS, located at the residence of Mr. Williams in St. Paul, Minnesota.

PUBLIC DOCUMENTS

California, Secretary of State. *Statement of Vote at General Election Held on November 6, 1934.* Sacramento, 1934.
———. *Statement of Vote at Primary Election Held on August 30, 1938.* Sacramento, 1938.
———. *Statement of Vote at General Election Held on November 8, 1938.* Sacramento, 1938.

215

BIBLIOGRAPHY

Iowa, Secretary of State. *State of Iowa—Official Register, 1939-1940.* Des Moines, 1939.
Minnesota, Secretary of State. *Legislative Manual of the State of Minnesota, 1933.* Minneapolis, 1933.
———. *Legislative Manual of the State of Minnesota, 1935.* Minneapolis, 1935.
———. *Legislative Manual of the State of Minnesota, 1937.* Minneapolis, 1937.
Oregon, Secretary of State. *Oregon Blue Book, 1935-1936.* Salem, 1937.
Wisconsin, Secretary of State. *Wisconsin Blue Book, 1935.* Madison, 1935.
———. *Wisconsin Blue Book, 1937.* Madison, 1937.
———. *Wisconsin Blue Book, 1940.* Madison, 1940.

UNPUBLISHED MATERIALS

Humola, Hulda F. "The Farmer-Labor Party in Minnesota, 1930-1938." Unpublished Master's Thesis, University of Chicago, 1944.
Mason, Bruce B. "American Political Protest, 1932-1936." Unpublished Ph.D. Dissertation, University of Texas, 1953.
Sarasohn, Stephen B. "The Struggle for Control of the American Labor Party, 1936-1948." Unpublished Master's Thesis, Columbia University, 1948.

216

INDEX

Agricultural Adjustment Administration: referenda on, 63; condemned by Farmers' Union affiliates, 63; mentioned, 33
Aikman, Douglas, 155-56
Alfonsi, Paul R., 178
Allen, Seymour E., 13
American Commonwealth Political Federation: and *Common Sense*, 40n; formed, 81-82; officers, 82, platform, 83-84; Communists excluded, 82-83; rationale expressed, 84-85; comments on, 85-87; political goals, 92-93; organizational activities, 94-95; and Minnesota Farmer-Labor party, 96-100, 104; and Olson, 97-100; comments on new-party goals of, 101-03; and Townsend movement, 103. *See also* Farmer-Labor convention of 1936
American Federation of Hosiery Workers, 25
American Institute of Public Opinion: poll on farmer-labor party support, 160; poll on National Progressives of America, 171-72
American Labor party: formed, 152, 159; supports Roosevelt, 159; 1937 New York City elections, 159; program, 159-60; leaders warn of possible new national party, 160; on National Progressives of America, 174
American Liberty League, 106-07
American Workers' Party, 10
Amlie, Thomas R.: on capitalism, 38-39; Farmer-Labor Political Federation chairman, 40; on constitutional revision, 41-42; and Wisconsin Progressive party, 47n; on Wisconsin Progressive party, 51; elected to Congress, 52-53; on Congressional progressives, 78; on political strategy, 78; Farmer-Labor Political Federation keynote speaker, 81; American Commonwealth Political Federation chairman, 82; opposes

Communists, 82-83; expresses American Commonwealth Political Federation rationale, 84-85; on radical political goals, 92-93; on Roosevelt's liberalism, 94; condemns Farmer-Labor convention, 108; supports Roosevelt, 113; criticizes Coughlin party, 141; mentioned, 80, 154

Bell, C. Jasper, 139
Benson, Elmer, 154, 158, 161
Berger, Mrs. Victor, 110
Berry, George L., 152
Bingham, Alfred M.: and *Common Sense*, 30n; Farmer-Labor Political Federation executive secretary, 40; hails native American radicals, 81; American Commonwealth Political Federation executive secretary, 82; as a political writer, 89-90; his *Insurgent America*, 90-92; letter to Olson, 99-100; condemns Browder's new party plea, 104; refuses to attend Farmer-Labor convention, 108; supports Roosevelt, 113
Black, Hugo, 154
Blanshard, Paul, 4
Bolens, Harry W., 181n
Bone, Homer, 66-67
Borah, William E., 67, 69, 126, 139
Bosch, John, 36, 82, 109-10
Brissenden, Paul, 4
Broughton, Charles, 53
Browder, Earl: calls for united front, 73; on farmer-labor party, 103-04; at Farmer-Labor convention, 109; on Union party, 146
Burdick, Usher L., 145

California Progressive party, 66, 165, 177, 181-82
Cantril, Hadley, 189
Casey, Joseph E., 152
Chase, Stuart, 4
Chavez, Denis, 69
Colby, Bainbridge, 93, 146

217

220

egy, 126, 128-29; assassination of, 129; mentioned, 12, 70
Lovett, Robert Morss, 4
Lubbell, Samuel, 192-93
Lundeen, Ernest, 80, 82, 158-59

McKaig, Ray, 66, 82-83
Mahoney, Bernard J., 151
Mahoney, William, 11n
Main, V. W., 138
Marcantonio, Vito, 80, 82
Maurer, James H., 4
Maverick, Maury, 154
Meiklejohn, Alexander, 4
Methodist Federation for Social Service, 125-26
Minnesota Farmer-Labor Association. See Minnesota Farmer-Labor party
Minnesota Farmer-Labor party: on national third party, 12; supports Roosevelt for President, 17; and Farmer-Labor Political Federation, 54-55; 1934 platform, 55-58; 1934 election campaign, 58-59; and American Commonwealth Political Federation, 96-100; calls for national Farmer-Labor party, 104-05; and Farmer-Labor convention, 107, 109-11; new national party activities after 1936, 158-59; on National Progressives of America, 174
Mundelein, George, 135
Murphy, Frank, 125, 161
Muste, A. J., 10

Nation, the, 3-4
National Farmer-Labor party, 12
National Farmers' Holiday Association. See Farm Holiday Association
National Farmers' Union. See Farmers' Union
National Industrial Recovery Act, 62
Nationalist party, 13
National Progressives of America: background of formation, 162-67; formed, 167, 171; poll on, 171-72; reaction to, 172-76; organizational activities and obstacles, 176-82; and Haight, 177,

181-82; and Iowa Farmer-Laborites, 177, 181-82; and Farmer-Labor Progressive Federation, 178; Wisconsin reaction to, 178-81; analysis of, 182-83; significance of defeat, 183
National Union for Social Justice: formed, 119; program, 119-21; organizational activities, 126-27; and Townsend movement, 140; political strategy of, 141; and Union party, 144; organ on 1936 election, 148. *See also* Charles E. Coughlin
Neibuhr, Reinhold, 4
New York Commonwealth Federation, 94
Nonpartisan League, 30
Norris, George W.: rejects third party action, 8, 11; supports Roosevelt for President, 17; on Democratic opposition to Cutting, 69-70; supports investigation of Farley, 70; and Progressive National Committee, 154; fears split of liberal forces, 172; quoted, 187; mentioned, 184
Nye, Gerald P.: on Senator Chavez, 69; on new-party strategy, 81; suggested as farmer-labor Presidential candidate, 104; mentioned, 70

O'Brien, Thomas C., 142, 147-48
O'Connell, Jerry, 67
O'Connell, William, 135n
Ohl, Henry, Jr., 46
Olson, Floyd B.: on farm and labor disgruntlement, 34-35; speech at Minnesota Farmer-Labor party convention, 55; on Minnesota Farmer-Labor party platform, 58; criticized by Farley, 71; on new party in 1936, 75; addresses Farmer-Labor Political Federation conference, 79; as radical leader, 97-98; and American Commonwealth Political Federation, 97-100; in favor of new political party, 98-99, 104; death of, 104n; on Farmer-Labor Presidential ticket, 107, 110

lin party, 125; hopes for national farmer-labor party, 160; on National Progressives of America, 174-75; mentioned, 22, 35. *See also* Norman Thomas
Social Security Act, 137-38
South Dakota Farmer-Labor Economic Federation, 44
Southern Tenant Farmers' Union, 67-68, 101

Talmadge, Eugene, 93, 102
Teigan, Henry: and Williams, 11n; on Wisconsin Progressive party, 51-52; on Coughlin, 116-17; mentioned, 159
Thomas, Elbert, 25
Thomas, Norman: rejects new-party idea, 16; League for Independent Political Action supports for President, 22, 24; favors liberal-leftist front, 71-72; on American Commonwealth Political Federation, 85; on Farmer-Labor convention, 112; on Union party, 146; on National Progressives of America, 174
Townley, A. C., 58
Townsend, Francis: and American Commonwealth Political Federation, 106; forms old age pension group, 135; opposed to third-party action, 138; threatens third-party action, 139; Congressional investigation of, 139-40; and G. L. K. Smith, 140; denies alliance with Coughlin, 142; mentioned, 156. *See also* Townsend movement
Townsend movement: on third-party action, 103; program, 135-36; and Roosevelt administration, 136-37; Chicago convention of, 138; and Union party, 144
Tugwell, Rexford, 68-69

Union party: discussed as left-of-center movement, 115-17; formed, 141-42; platform, 142-43; and Townsend movement, 144; and National Union for Social Justice, 144; and Farm Holiday Association, 145; comments on, 146-47; assessments of campaign of, 155-57
United Textile Workers, 25

Vandenberg, Arthur H., 70
Veterans' bonus, 70
Villard, Oswald Garrison, 4, 21, 40, 113

Vladeck, B. C., 4
Wagner Act, 61-62, 70
Waldman, Louis, 108
Wallace, Henry A., 35, 125
Walsh, Frank P., 154
Washington Commonwealth Federation, 66-67
Webb, Frank E., 12, 14
Weber, Vin, 57
Weiss, Carl, Jr., 129
Whitney, A. F., 41-42
Williams, Howard Y.: League for Independent Political Action executive secretary, 4; and Minnesota Farmer-Labor party, 11n, 54-55; sees necessity of new party, 21-22; Farmer-Labor Political Federation national organizer, 40; American Commonwealth Political Federation national organizer, 82; on radical political goals, 93; proposes Gerald Nye for President, 104; on Farmer-Labor Presidential ticket, 108; Farmer-Labor convention keynote speaker, 109; on Union party, 147; mentioned, 78, 113, 159
Wilson, George I., 13
Winant, John G., 137
Wirds, John F., 82
Wisconsin Co-operative Milk Pool, 36, 46
Wisconsin Farmer-Labor Progressive Federation. *See* Wisconsin Progressive party
Wisconsin Farm Holiday Association, 46
Wisconsin Federation of Labor, 46
Wisconsin Progressive party; situations fostering formation of, 44-46; formed, 47; platform, 47-

50; leadership, 49; and Roosevelt, 49; national ambitions of, 50; comments on, 50-53; and Socialist party, 51; 1934 election campaign, 52-53; and Farmer-Labor Progressive Federation,

95-96, 178, 180; troubles in 1938, 178-81; 1938 election, 181; mentioned, 100

Zimmerman, Peter, 67
Zionchek, Marion, 25